Humphrey Bog

David Thomson is, among many other things, author of *The New Biographical Dictionary of Film*, now in its fourth edition. His recent books include a biography of Nicole Kidman, completing and editing *Fan Tan* (a novel started by Marlon Brando and Donald Cammell) and *The Whole Equation: A History of Hollywood*. His latest work is the acclaimed *Have You Seen...? A Personal Introduction to 1,000 Films*. Born in London, he now lives in San Francisco.

PENGUIN BOOKS – GREAT STARS

David Thomson

Humphrey Bogart

Ingrid Bergman

Gary Cooper

Bette Davis

Humphrey Bogart

DAVID THOMSON

Photo research by Lucy Gray

GREAT STARS

For Sean Arnold

PENGUIN BOOKS

Published by the Penguin Group
Penguin Books Ltd, 80 Strand, London WC2R ORL, England
Penguin Group (USA) Inc., 375 Hudson Street, New York, New York 10014, USA
Penguin Group (Canada), 90 Eglinton Avenue East, Suite 700, Toronto, Ontario, Canada M4P 2Y3
(a division of Pearson Penguin Canada Inc.)
Penguin Ireland, 25 St Stephen's Green, Dublin 2, Ireland
(a division of Penguin Books Ltd)
Penguin Group (Australia), 250 Camberwell Road, Camberwell, Victoria 3124, Australia
(a division of Pearson Australia Group Pty Ltd)
Penguin Books India Pvt Ltd, 11 Community Centre, Panchsheel Park, New Delhi – 110 017, India
Penguin Group (NZ), 67 Apollo Drive, Rosedale, North Shore 0632, New Zealand
(a division of Pearson New Zealand Ltd)
Penguin Books (South Africa) (Pty) Ltd, 24 Sturdee Avenue, Rosebank, Johannesburg 2196, South Africa

Penguin Books Ltd, Registered Offices: 80 Strand, London WC2R ORL, England

www.penguin.com

First published 2009
1

Set in Garamond MT 12.5/15.5pt
Typeset by Palimpsest Book Production Limited,
Grangemouth, Stirlingshire
Printed in England by Clays Ltd, St Ives plc

ISBN: 978-1-846-14076-1

www.greenpenguin.co.uk

Penguin Books is committed to a sustainable future
for our business, our readers and our planet.
The book in your hands is made from paper
certified by the Forest Stewardship Council.

Look, I'm hardly pretty, he seems to say. I sound like gravel; I look rough and tough; and, honest, I don't give you the soft, foolish answers the pretty boys will give you. You may not like what I say, but you better believe it. I know, I'm a star in a funny kind of way, but not because I set out to be one, and not because I sold out. Honest.

It all works as a speech until you look at the imploring eyes, longing to be believed, trying to believe.

Actors should keep in work as steadily as possible – that or drink make the best recipe for avoiding eye contact or any friction of the soul with that treacherous shadow to which they may find themselves attached, their image. In the case of Humphrey Bogart – 'Bogie', they used to say, out of respect – the shadow was a rugged ideal. It was everything he wanted to be – which means everything a kid from World War I could dream of. We are talking about an age of such idealism that it can look foolish now. Yet when his time came, at last, and when he had the most glorious, obedient sexpot in tow a guy in his forties and losing his hair could ever imagine, why 'Bogie' took the whole package for a while, on the chin. But then he soured, as if to admit the ideal was a killer, more than any man could survive.

He died short of sixty, and convention said it was from the smoking and the booze and the not taking care of himself. Maybe it was just possessing too much irony or common sense to endure being a pliable ghost in strangers' dreams – 'Bogie'. But then for thirty years after his death, that image grew clearer and more immaculate – it became an emblem of American cinema and stoicism, and inasmuch as Rick in *Casablanca* stood for initial American wariness or neutrality coming to realize the justice of the war, why Bogart fell in line with what we would one day call 'the best generation'. The one that knew the difference between a hill of beans and a mountain of dead bodies. The one that winced if you said 'best' and had a suitably cynical wise-crack waiting on the big word. And for twenty years or so, Bogie was untouchable, not just the best but dismissive and corrosive enough to strip out all the pomp, smugness and medals that went with it. He made the kids' films of America seem grown up.

He was good enough to have played Ernest Hemingway for real. But don't forget that Hemingway shot himself at the dawn of that age when Americans started to shoot their own heroes, as if the cult of being best was getting out of hand.

He was named Humphrey De Forest Bogart, and he was born on Christmas Day, 1899, to parents who featured in the New York Blue Book. Louise Brooks, who knew him quite well in the mid-20s, saw a 'Humphrey' (a very respectable name) and a rather slight, morbidly beautiful dark-haired youth who was trying to behave as his family expected. The father was a successful surgeon, though a man who went in great pain from a riding accident and who was accustomed to inject himself with morphine when the pain became too much. He provided the same service for his wife, Maud Humphrey, who was a very successful illustrator of children's books. Her professional income was said to be $50,000 a year, and she sometimes chose Humphrey as one of her angelic models.

The family had a large house in Manhattan (just off Riverside Drive) and a country house at Seneca Point on Candaigua Lake in the western reach of upstate New York. It was there that the boy found his lifelong love of sailing. He was known for tidy looks and perfect manners, and there is little early sign that his need to model for his mother's lucrative but idealized drawings made him more sceptical or critical. More than nearly any other film star, Bogart came from real class and grew up without finding need or reason to challenge that slightly anti-American distinction. He spoke very well, and you can hear that sometimes in his famous roles. For although this Bogart mixed with people like Ugarte, Eddie the drunk and Brigid O'Shaughnessy, still the actor had a quiet, orderly respect for protocol and grammar that contrasted nicely with his tart tongue. Rick has knocked around the world, but he has been educated. Think of Marlowe's meeting with General Sternwood in the hot-house at the start of *The Big Sleep* – he will be drenched in his own sweat; he utters some sour one-liners; he knows the underworld, it seems. Yet he knows Sternwood's world, too, and he impresses the general as a man to be saluted. After all, his Philip Marlowe is a modern knight, serving the 'good' for a very modest daily wage, often doubting the imitations of virtue, but always seeing it when it is for real – as in the forlorn figure of Harry Jones (Elisha Cook Jr). This Bogart may have given up on the world of class and etiquette, but he remembers it, and he never really betrays it. What I'm trying to say is that if Bogart had suddenly been cast as an American gentleman – FDR, Dean Acheson, or Faulkner – he'd have carried it off. His Marlowe – a figure of immense caustic integrity – is not so far from figures like Bulldog Drummond and even James Bond. In the great turmoil of that film's story, Marlowe and his forward motion can be trusted. Marlowe, we should remember, was the creation of a failed but dreamy English public schoolboy who cherished Edwardian codes of honour and service.

If you want another point of reference think of Gore Vidal, a natural wit, glowingly intelligent, and plainly from class. Of course, Vidal never needed university, and never embraced Bogie's macho mannerisms. But Vidal made up his own lines.

Still, Bogart had one advantage over Vidal: beyond dispute, he had failed. He went to the Trinity Church prep school, but his marks were so poor that he was only advanced to Phillips Academy at Andover (a top school, and his father's) on probation. Alas, in his year there he failed to raise his scores and he was asked to withdraw from the school. His parents were not pleased and they arranged a job for him, working in a naval architect's office. But Humphrey was tired of trying to please parents for whom he had little love. And so on 5 May 1918, ignoring their plan, he went to Brooklyn and joined the Navy.

No one has ever claimed that Bogart's service was distinctive. He was appointed to the *Leviathan* and two days later the Armistice was declared. He was then posted to the *Santa Olivia* and he served until the summer of 1919, but not even Bogart spoke of action or interest. All that remains is the assumption that he suffered a damaged lip during the service and had minor surgery to mend it. Louise Brooks observed that he had 'a most beautiful mouth', but then she saw the scar at one corner where a scallop of skin was sewed up, leaving just a small scar. She believed that this operation occurred only when he went into films. But there are biographies that assume it occurred in the Navy (perhaps in a struggle with a drunken prisoner) and that Bogart's own father did the adjustment.

I wonder. There are films where Bogart plays with his own mouth, and some where he nearly lisps. Yet in truth it is very hard to see the scar. Lauren Bacall, his great love, seems not to have noticed it. Among all the speculation over the lip or the mouth, we have to preserve the possibility that Bogart invented it and would allude to it occasionally as if invoking magic. A moveable scar, a secret trigger – a thing that let his mouth go nasty or mean. As Captain Queeg in *The Caine Mutiny* – one of the most studious pieces of acting in Bogart's career, and quite impressive – the lisp is more pronounced than anywhere else, and we are meant to hear it as a sign of flaw and even cowardice.

After all, it wasn't a million miles from the tightlipped male humour of Bogart and Howard Hawks that a fellow might get kissed a lot by solicitous women if they heard he had a numb lip that needed warming up. It is the sort of routine that Tony Curtis runs on Marilyn Monroe in *Some Like It Hot*.

Bogart was released from the Navy on 18 June 1919 as a seaman second class. Twenty years later, he made the film, *The Roaring Twenties*, at Warner Brothers. It's not a bad picture, a gangster story in which Bogart plays Jimmy Cagney's enemy (and earned maybe a quarter of Cagney's salary). In that twenty-year period (his youth), he became increasingly embittered and more than ever certain of his own failure. Of course, he was under contract as an actor, latterly at Warners, on a sliding scale that would raise his pay to $1,750 a week by 1942 (when the contract terminated). He was kept in work: he made thirty pictures in those contract years, two of them on loan-out, but the first at Warners. And in all those reels of film, he was sent to jail, executed or removed in some gun battle more times than he could remember, or forget. He was his own 'dead end', an emphatic warning, without subtlety or a hint of redemption. The audience was trained to dislike him or disapprove, albeit in a loyalist way – for he was one of Warners' favourite snarling hoodlums, a guy you could trust not to trust. His response, in 1940, was to write a fan-magazine article, 'Why Hollywood Hates Me', which trotted out all the familiar bromides: his fierce independence, his dislike of flattery or adulation, and the kind of professionalism that did his dirty deeds without complaining. Don't worry about me, he said. He'd be all right, because he had never fallen for the lies of Hollywood, the exploitation of people and the routine of telling stories about a fantasy world. More than that, he had a habit at parties, as he got drunk, of reciting his very worst reviews, and at such times no doubt he exaggerated the rasp of his voice so that sometimes people felt they could hear self-hatred. It was only on hearing Bogart, that theatre director Arthur Hopkins cast him as gangster Duke Mantee in *The Petrified Forest*, his first great turning point – and only fifteen years after he had started.

So what did he want? For he had chosen to be an actor. In the same years hundreds and thousands of young Americans sought to be actors, and there are names we will never know or remember. Because they got no notices, or roles even. Because their performances were confined to the one room they lived in, the mirror or the shower. Humphrey Bogart was an esteemed character actor. He delivered a set image much in demand at Warners. In his time, he had a couple of lead parts at the studio. And in the end, everyone agreed that fate had uncovered him so that suddenly – with the coming of war – he became a star. But he had worked on stage and screen with people like Elisha Cook Jr who never rose beyond the level of beautiful bit parts. America recognized Cook's squashed baby face without knowing the name. But Bogart was known by name and personality. He was famous for his snarl and a nasty attitude that went with it. And there were those who reported him unpleasant and cruel – as well as cowardly if he could see Cagney's bullets headed for his stomach. But there were a few like Louise Brooks, who reckoned he was just a softie hurt at being disliked and a drunk who was inclined to fall asleep on you.

In the 1920s, as far as research can ascertain, Bogart appeared in ten plays. Some ran as many as 200 or 300 performances, but others were off in a week or two. He was usually the ingénu or a cad, a partner in tennis or romance, handsomely dressed, gracious, well-spoken – until he made the voice go harsh – and unlike anyone else. He had learned that much at least, along with membership at most Broadway speakeasies. He made a friend of Clifton Webb (they were together in one play). He got Mary Boland to tolerate him, even though

On stage, 1921, with Shirley Booth

he forgot his lines with her once. And he came on board as a replacement in a Ruth Gordon play so that the actress knew he was inferior, but decent and doing his best.

There were plenty of women in his life. Louise Brooks was one of them, and she was struck that Bogart had little feeling for real life. He tended to fall for girls he was acting with. In one play, he got into a fight with actress Helen Menken. Some scenery fell on her. She tore him off a strip. He booted her and she hit him. Within days they had a marriage licence to show for it. It didn't last, but he fell for Mary Philips because of the way she walked away from him on stage. It was provocative, he thought, and it had some stealth meant for him alone. That was two wives and two more would be Mayo Methot and Lauren Bacall – it was as if he could hardly do a pretend kiss without being led astray. He liked to be thought of as a tough guy, a man of the world, but four times he fell in love under the lights. You have to see how chronic a dreamer there was there – and you have to see how far he was hiding that guy during the decades of his morose act.

There is a good deal more that comes unexpectedly to light, and which gets only a few pages in the Bogart biographies. Humphrey plainly felt at one time that by going on the stage he was defying or rebuking family expectations. But then the very family went into strange decline. In fact, Bogart had strong feelings for his father – and very few for his mother. But in the early 30s, the father sank. He lost a lot of money in the Crash. His health deteriorated rapidly. And he broke up with his wife or decided to live apart from her. The wife's career declined at the same time. The father died in 1934, at the age of sixty-six, leaving debts of over $10,000 that Humphrey made good on. Then in 1937, Humphrey's younger sister, Kay – a model and a beauty – died from peritonitis. The other sister, Pat, was divorced and entered upon a long period of depressive illness that included hospitalization. And so, by the late 30s, the family was broken with Humphrey – himself often out of money – the vital support for them all. It would be going too far to say that this made for self-pity. Indeed, I don't think the world at large knew too much about the family story – though Edward G. Robinson, a colleague at Warners, did remark on the family disturbance. Still, if you look at Bogart's face in the 20s and the 30s, you will see a development of something rueful, tragic and older than he seemed. For example, at the time of *Casablanca*, Bogart was only 44 – the age of Tom Cruise in 2006 on *Mission Impossible: 3*. Yet consider how much older or more pained Bogart seems. Drink accounted for a lot, but by the late 30s, this was a man with heavy sorrows and a reliable record of bad luck or of seeming 'doomed'. It was set too deep to be erased when Bogart had made it and could claim to be happy.

It's hard now, and not very useful, to assess Bogart's potential, on stage or screen, in the early 30s. Elia Kazan was a young stage manager on one of the plays, *Chrysalis*, and he judged it a terrible production, in which the players' ignorance of what to do matched that of the writer. This was 1932 and *Chrysalis* was a melodrama by Rose Albert Porter. Its cast included Margaret Sullavan, Bogart, Osgood Perkins and Elisha Cook Jr, and in one scene Bogart had to make love to Sullavan. As Kazan saw it, Bogart was playing a 'patent leather parlour sheikh', a shallow womanizer.

No one admiring Bogart would think he could get away with that. The instinctive breakthrough on *To Have and Have Not* is that the considerable romantic reservoir in Bogart is not brave or outgoing. It must be invaded by the daring or insolence of a woman. He is too shy, or too impressed by love, to act it out. The girl is going to have to woo him. He may respond then, thus allowing her reward – it's better when two of us do it. So Bogart was being exposed in something like *Chrysalis*, thrust beyond his means or sensible casting. In 1932, not even Kazan saw what was waiting, or what might one day be discovered. And here's a woeful condition of acting: that players may be helpless in the process of their own rescue or salvation. So history has no verdict on Bogart the stage actor. He failed to impress or last. I suspect that Bogart always lacked the taste or the energy to be immensely outgoing – in the way that roles like Willy Loman or Hickey in *The Iceman Cometh* require. But plays like that were not far away, and surely it's easier to see and hear Bogart in that vein. In 1952, Kazan would direct Lee J. Cobb in the premiere of *Death of a Sales-man*. It was around the time Bogart won his Oscar in *The African Queen*. In his book, Kazan admits that the writer Arthur Miller always felt that Loman should have been someone smaller than Cobb.

Bogart as Loman is a dream that never happened, but actors think on such things naturally because they are always waiting for such magic to strike. And just a few years later, something like this happens with a play called *The Petrified Forest*. It will open at the Broadhurst Theatre in New York on 7 January 1935, written by Robert Sherwood, and produced by Gilbert Miller and Arthur Hopkins.

It is a strange play, set in the desolate Black Mesa Bar B-Q in Arizona. We find Alan Squire there, an exhausted intellectual beaten down by the world. The Black Mesa is filled with failures and losers, except for a woman, Gabby Maple, who dreams of Paris and being a painter. Enter Duke Mantee, an escaped convict and a fuse paper for this very poised melodrama. Mantee was written as a fig-ure of threatening violence and disruptive menace. Leslie Howard, the movie star, was set as Alan Squire, lending an effete, wistful European fatalism to the character. Peggy Conklin was Gabby. And it was Bogart's abrasive voice that got him the part of Duke. Adding to that, he wore a pallid make-up and two days of going without shaving to show a lifelong prisoner kept from the sun. He had a brutish self-inflicted haircut and a shuffling walk that had lost any memory of freedom.

The Petrified Forest

The play was an immediate hit, and Bogart was part of it. Howard's role was larger and central, but Bogart's appearance was riveting – it seemed to remind audiences of John Dillinger, a hot news item – and the box office reported customers seeking front-row seats to study the look on Mantee's face. There was immediate talk of film rights, with Warners in the lead – it was a kind of gangster picture and they had worked happily with Leslie Howard in the past. Jack Warner went to see the play himself and concluded that the death of Squire was very close to the public mood at that moment. Warners paid $110,000 for the screen rights (next year the picture rights on *Gone With the Wind* would be sold for just $50,000).

Howard was vital to the deal, and he had said at first that he thought Bogart should be retained to play Duke Mantee. On the closing night of the play, Howard had called Bogart out of the cast line for a special bow. The two men were on good terms, but Bogart was wise to be wary. Peggy Conklin was abandoned by the studio for Bette Davis, and in the summer of 1935 – before Bogart had a contract – *Variety* ran a story that the studio was going to go with Edward G. Robinson as Mantee. Bogart got drunk and slipped into self-pity – same old Bogart luck. But he was wrong. Leslie Howard drew the line: 'No Bogart, no deal'. He was in, on a one-picture contract at $750 a week. It was real money for a featured part.

Word spread at the Burbank studio, and visitors came

by to see Bogart work. Of course, it was Hollywood, and the front office was slow to make up its mind over the play's bleak ending or a happier resolution where Squire lived! In the event, *The Petrified Forest* was a prestige production – let him die! And when it opened, the picture did very well, with Bogart getting his best ever notices and – a late decision – promotion to co-lead status in the billing.

Better still, weeks before the public saw *The Petrified Forest*, Warners were throwing contracts at Bogart. In early January 1936, he signed on with the studio, a five-year deal, lasting until 1941. He was starting at $550 a week, and if he got all his renewals he'd be at $1,750 a week at the end. This was not a star contract, but it was the reward for a featured player. Inevitably, this meant that he would be based in Hollywood. And while no one could have guessed it at the time, it was the end to his stage career.

The years of that contract were not really happy. Like many people under service at Warners – men and women – Bogart became irked at his very limited opportunities and bored by the ways the studio could find for him to die. He was never comfortable in Los Angeles. His second marriage – to Mary Philips – broke apart in 1936 when she saw her big opportunity: being cast as Cora Papadakis opposite Richard Barthelmess in the stage version of James M. Cain's *The Postman Always Rings Twice*. That 'daring' play didn't run very long and Bogart's estimate – that Mary wasn't exactly the wicked sexpot it needed – seemed to hold water. So Bogart met and began to go around with Mayo Methot, the woman who would be his third wife – a drunk, a loudmouth, a fighter yet a pretty good singer. His front hair began to fall out, so he was compelled to resort to a toupee. There were moments in the late 30s when Bogart really didn't look too good.

How was he to know in 1936 or 7 that Betty Perske was only 12? If you'd said that, he might have been shocked enough to hit you in the mouth for being so dirty-minded. He was a drunk, belligerent and often in a foul temper, but he tried to be a gentleman.

It was enough at Warner Brothers that Bogart should be considered a punching bag for Cagney, Edward G. Robinson and George Raft. Along with Paul Muni, these guys had been stars for years. They had much better contracts and they had their brand 'image': Cagney was Irish, sweet-natured in person but a dangerous imp on screen, a guy who moved as if he had been hot-wired; Robinson was a sweetie, an art collector, from Bucharest originally, a worldly fellow – but very nasty on screen; and George Raft was another dancer and a ladies' man, the real-life friend to gangsters like Bugsy Siegel. As for Muni, he was older, famous as a very studied actor, and the natural player for biopics and historical tributes. Still, it happened that, just as Bogart really arrived at the studio, he was swept aside by another signing.

Black Legion

Errol Flynn was ten years younger than Bogart and a lot more beautiful. He came from Tasmania with an easy manner and a crowd of women following him. In a rush, he became a costume star – *Captain Blood, The Charge of the Light Brigade* and *The Adventures of Robin Hood*. It was hard to be grudging about Flynn, but Bogart knew – like everyone else – that if you tried putting him in period clothes he looked lost and laughable. A couple of times at Warners he tried to be a cowboy but no one ever believed in dressing him up, putting a sword in his hand or having him leap the length of castle staircases. Plus Flynn got as many of the young actresses and groupies as he could handle, while Bogart (in 1938) married for the third time to an actress he nicknamed 'Sluggy' – because she was likely to hit him in their many quarrels. Mayo Methot was a seething personality who saw her career closing down. So she drank and she prompted him to drink. They became famous for being thrown out of bars and having the cops called. She sounds disastrous, yet of the first three wives in his life she held by far the strongest power over him. Indeed, there were even observers who reckoned the tough actor needed to be rescued from her and retained maudlin memories long after she had been replaced by a modern princess.

Warner Brothers was an effective studio. It had had Darryl Zanuck as one production chief, and he was succeeded by Hal Wallis – these were top executives by any Hollywood test. Further, the studio had a number of very talented producer figures – Henry Blanke, Robert Lord, David Lewis and Jerry Wald. The studio was known as a man's world with gangster stories and costume epics leading the way. But it was also the home to Bette Davis and Olivia de Havilland, the two actresses who would do more to overthrow the contract system than any of the disobedient actors. It was a studio known for sharp writing and very polished directors – Raoul Walsh, Michael Curtiz, William Dieterle and John Huston. It is true that Bogart was allowed to mark time there, but it is unlikely that any other studio in the late 30s would have known what to do with his odd talent. Truth to tell, Humphrey Bogart found himself (or drifted into a more acute version of himself) just as the familiar crime genre took some unexpected turns. But there is no evidence that anyone at the studio could have predicted that course of events, or understood it any better than Bogart himself. One day he was the guy they went to if George Raft said no. The next he was the fellow who left Raft looking like a simpleton.

And even when he had a chance to excel, the picture might be a touch too bold for the public and the studio. Take *Black Legion*, which may be the least known major work Bogart would ever do. This is nothing less than an indictment of the Ku Klux Klan, and a portrait of a very ordinary American worker, Frank Taylor (Bogart), who is offended when he loses his job to a man named 'Dombrowski'. Although it is not pointedly set in the South and does not directly involve race, still *Black*

Legion understands the kind of thinking that is ready to blame others for hard times. It also employed a fairly accurate version of the Klan's oath-taking procedure.

Written and produced by Robert Lord, with Abem Finkel and William Wister Hains also working on the script, *Black Legion* was directed by the Archie Mayo who had done *The Petrified Forest.* The Taylor character is neither excused nor redeemed by the picture. Instead, we see how easily his sense of grievance is led into organized reaction and then violence. And Bogart is quite brilliant in the scenes where his character takes up a gun and kills for the first time. It's still disconcerting that the film is so little known – as if the reluctance to offend had tempered the studio's courage in taking it on. Even at the time, Warners talked about it as if Paul Muni might have been the more sensible lead actor. But that's a way of saying how good and unsympathetic Bogart is. It's easy to imagine other studio players dodging the lead role here and the film does not have a very distinguished supporting cast.

In the *New York Post*, Archer Winston found Bogart dynamic and stirring. 'The role is one which demands the talents of a Muni or a Robinson . . . No more B pix for Bogart!' In England Graham Greene said, 'It is an intelligent film because the director and script-writer know where the real horror lies: the real horror is not in the black robes and the skull emblems, but in the knowledge that these hide the weak and commonplace faces you have met over the counter and minding the next machine.' Greene compared it with Fritz Lang's *Fury*, and even if that was the better film he believed Bogart had done admirable work. To this day, it is a picture that has Bogart's front hair combed straight across his head – without the jaunty widow's peak. And if only for that reason, he looks like a lost soul, and a real actor.

Such things were noticed, and Bogart could grumble if the studio never really got behind the problematic *Black Legion*. On other occasions, he was expected to assist the cause of other stars – more important and far more troublesome. Bette Davis was a Warners contract player, and a star. She was younger than Bogart (by nine years), but she was a great deal more forthright on her ambitions as an actress. Although she had won an Oscar in *Dangerous* (in 1935), she had contempt for that picture and for a lot of what Warners offered her. It was when she was expected to play a female lumberjack in *God's Country and the Woman* that she rebelled. She took a trip to London and refused to answer her contract calls. As a result, Warners took action against her in the London courts – and won. The actress was humiliated and ordered home to do her work.

In fact, Warners learned a lesson. They picked up the bill for her costs and they offered her the lead in *Marked Woman*. With a screenplay by Robert Rossen and Abem Finkel, this is a story of the ill fate of prostitutes under the empire of a gangster like Lucky Luciano. In the film, the boss was named Johnny Vanning, but Eduardo Ciannelli would play the part. Davis was Mary

Dwight Strauber, a vivacious, brave hooker who suffers being defaced in order to give testimony to the D.A. – David Graham, a figure based on the New York lawyer Thomas E. Dewey, and a role being lined up for Humphrey Bogart. Indeed, for Davis, Bogart's presence was an extra sweetener for he was thought to be on the rise. (And to please Bogart Mayo Methot was cast as another of the naughty girls – though her best scene proved to be one where she gazed in the mirror and lamented the loss of her looks.)

Lloyd Bacon directed what was, for Warners, an unusual examination of crime as seen through women's eyes. For the climax of the film, Davis had to be savagely beaten up. She went to make-up to sit for their version of the repair job and decided that it was too genteel. Instead, she went out to a doctor and explained what had happened to the character. 'Now, dress me up so it shows,' she said. The result allegedly horrified the studio – they thought their star had had a real accident – but they soon saw the shock value of this new look. Moreover, it has to be said that *Marked Woman* breaks through many of the conventions of the crime picture. Davis knows it's a good story and she is especially pretty under threat. The flat part of the movie is Bogart who makes 'David Graham' all too plainly a state official, instead of a man who might be moved by Mary's courage. Years later, Pauline Kael would point out how official position was a handicap to a man like Bogart. But the pity is that just a modest script adjustment could have allowed some more feeling between the two of them

It's hard to know how Bogart and Davis got on: they made four films together, but Bogart always said that he felt overawed by her and her status. Yet there's a hint of chemistry in *Marked Woman* as well as the fact that, later on in life, she would marry Gary Merrill, one of the actors with a Bogart-like look and manner. It's more intriguing to wonder whether she gave him tips on how to handle a dumb studio system.

One other picture deserves mention from the late 30s – the most significant event of his career to date. Sidney Kingsley's play *Dead End* opened in New York in October 1935. It was a sensation in which the great set – by Norman Bel Geddes – took pride of place. It was a play about the flagrant juxtaposition of rich and poor in urban life, and about the way a young architect dreams of reconciliation. For this is a city where luxury apartment buildings and slum tenements alike come to sip the fetid waters of the river. The set comprised a stretch of waterfront – the dead end – with a pool of water in which the wild kids might swim.

Samuel Goldwyn saw the play with his favourite director William Wyler and they had agreed to make it before the applause died away. Goldwyn paid $165,000 for the movie rights, and he put Lillian Hellman to work to produce a screenplay. The architect (Joel McCrea) has a childhood friend who comes back to the neigh-bourhood as a gangster – Baby Face Martin. Naturally enough, Goldwyn thought of Warner Brothers as the place where he could find Baby Face.

His dream was to have Jimmy Cagney, who had certainly done the good kid–bad kid routine in New York stories. But Cagney was in a temporary dispute with Warners and the studio was unwilling to jeopardize its legal status. Whereupon the choice fell on George Raft. But Raft read the script and turned sensitive. 'I told Mr Goldwyn how I would like to play the part. I want a scene where I tell the kids how bad my life is. Just look at me crawling around like a rat, hiding. You don't want to hide all your life. Make something of yourself.' When his mother (Marjorie Main, looking haggard from exhaustion, but only a few years older than Bogart) accuses Baby Face of cowardice, the play had him just angry but Raft wanted tears and a sign that he knows mother knows best.

So Bogart, ready to dare the worst in the role, would be Baby Face Martin – his face rigid from plastic surgery, his insecurities tossed back and forth by his mother and his girlfriend, Francey (Claire Trevor).

It was a $900,000 budget, and Goldwyn was ready to be squeezed. To get Bogart for five weeks, he had to pay Warners $10,000 for the loan-out. In turn, Warners' normal payment of five weeks on Bogart's contract was $3,250. As loan-outs went, this was a modest exploitation. But it helped Bogart put on Baby Face's fixed sneer.

Dead End introduced a gang of urchins (Leo Gorcey,

Huntz Hall and others) who would become known as the Bowery Boys or the Dead End Kids. It was also famous for Richard Day's magnificent yet implausible set, Gregg Toland's photography, and as one more of those American works brooding on the unjust social contract in the 1930s. It was nominated for Best Picture, but lost out to *The Life of Emile Zola*, a Warner Brothers biopic with Paul Muni as the French writer. In the same film, Joseph Schildkraut won the supporting actor Oscar for his rendering of Dreyfuss. Bogart was not nominated, but he can't have been too far away (Claire Trevor was nominated as supporting actress). In costumes by Omar Kiam, Bogart helped pioneer the gangster style of shirts darker than his suits. He had never looked more striking or elegant. Any worry over his hair was settled by the way Baby Face wore a fedora for most of the picture.

It's a contrived, stagy picture; it always was. The great coup of having luxury apartments overlook slums is too forced, too adjacent. In reality, such rough seams are kept out of sight. Graham Greene noticed this at the time, just as he caught the panache and the real social revelation in Bogart's gangster. 'Bogart pauses several times in his talk, as if sinking into the despair of his character. And almost for the first time we notice the ruefulness in his eyes.' Greene wrote:

I'm doubtful whether this interweaving of plots, which ends in the timid brother giving himself up, in the housepainter realizing he loves the sister, in the gangster's death from the housepainter's bullet, is wise. It gives too melodramatic a tone to the dead end: some emotion of grief, fear, passion happens to everybody, when surely the truth is nothing ever really happens at all. It remains one of the best pictures of the year – but what we remember is the gangster, the man who in a sentimental moment returns to the old home. He wants to see his mother and his girl: sentiment is mixed with pride – he's travelled places; he shows his shirtsleeve –'Look – silk, twenty bucks.' And in two memorable scenes sentimentality turns savage in him. His mother slaps his face ('just stay away and leave us alone and die'), his girl is diseased and on the streets. This is the finest performance Bogart has ever given – the ruthless sentimentalist who has melodramatized himself from the start (the start is there before your eyes in the juvenile gangsters) up against the truth, and the fine flexible direction supplies a background of beetle-ridden staircases and mud and mist.

Greene's passionate insight is very exciting: it addresses the Bogart we know now, but not the one most people saw in 1937. It leaves you wondering if Bogart could ever have played grown men in Graham Greene novels. It surely leaves the modern reader wondering what he was doing at Warners for the next few years in things like *Swing Your Lady*, *Crime School*, *Racket Busters*, *The Oklahoma Kid* and *Invisible Stripes*. And that is just a selection. Between *Dead End* and *High Sierra*, Bogart made another eighteen pictures, and the sum total of those years served to scatter his image and his reputation, not to focus or enhance it. It's easy to be fond of Warner Brothers in this era, and it's hard to disapprove of the regimen that tells everyone to work hard and get experience. But if Warners was run by brilliant businessmen with a sense of story and character – what in the world was happening?

Actors do not always know what is right for them in the way that history makes clear. At the same time, actors can learn in the process of their own work. The most intriguing thing about watching *Dead End* now is to feel Bogart – on the edge of Baby Face's truly malignant soul – beginning to sniff out a much more honourable pessimism. It was observed at Warners that, more than most actors, Bogart was a reader – and it's reasonable to suspect that he was trying to feel out the different tones available to tough guys.

We know that Bogart complained to the studio bosses about his treatment. Yet at Warners, those bosses were accustomed to that sort of grumbling. Bogart took several suspensions – moments when he declined to work on a particular project. But he seems fairly amenable. One of his agents, Noll Gurney, at the Myron Selznick office, wrote to Jack Warner:

There is no question in his [Bogart's] mind that you are the one motion picture producer to have faith in him and putting him into *Petrified Forest* . . . Humphrey points out that perhaps your attitude . . . is affected by the fact that after *Petrified*

Forest he did eight or nine unimportant pictures – this was not his fault because *Black Legion* proved that he was worthy of not only your faith in him but that *Petrified Forest* had justified his being in more important pictures . . .

I do wish, Jack, that you could see your way clear to reconsider this matter . . . [Humphrey] has cooperated one hundred per cent with your studio, has given nobody any trouble and . . . has devoted much of his time to the radio and publicity departments.

There were problems between Bogart and George Raft – and why not? Looked at now, their odd juxtaposition (they are meant to be brothers in *They Drive by Night*) is like a curse imposed on them by an author to see which of them will yelp first or seek a way out. Raft's real name was Ranft – he was half-German and half-Italian, and all low-life. He had boxed and there was a rumour that that expertise had led gangsters to like him. He was also a skilled, fast-paced dancer, with the impassive, cruel gaze that suited some people's idea of the tango. He knew gangsters, make no mistake. He kept company with Ben 'Bugsy' Siegel: in turn that added to George's rep as a hard case and it fostered the story that Siegel really fancied himself in movies. Anyone from Humphrey's class was going to see Raft as riff-raff, but in the mid-30s Warners had acquired him from Paramount, and they showed every sign of meaning to build his status. He was good-looking. Some apparently liked him. Surely it would have worked if he wasn't such a chump.

And just as surely, George Raft helped Bogie compose his view of the world, the one that identified him.

But Raft did not act alone. John Huston was beginning to think about Bogart. Huston was thirty-four in 1940, and he was the son of the actor Walter Huston. He was an unusually adventurous young man, self-taught in everything from poker to literature. He had accompanied his father on the travelling theatre circuit. He had been a boxer and an officer in the Mexican cavalry. And as an ironic storyteller, he had slipped into screenwriting in the early 30s. He had been married twice. He had been the driver in a fatal traffic accident that was successfully hushed up. There is even some suspicion that he was part of a strange circle of art-lovers who may have had some influence on the notorious Black Dahlia murder of 1947. (This is not idle rumour-mongering. Huston and the man who is still the leading suspect, Dr George Hodel, had been married to the same woman.)

Of course, we know John Huston now as the film director – the writer and the actor. But in the late 30s, he was more clearly a wanderer and a jack of many trades – as well as a man with a warm sympathy for scoundrels and rogues. I do not say this as a way of being funny or clever. Huston often spoke about his fondness for villains – it is no small thing in the Bogart story. And from the moment they met, Bogart was in awe of the younger man's knowledge, his decisiveness and his indifference to others.

Huston was a deft screenwriter. He worked on *Jezebel* (1938), a very successful Bette Davis picture, and in the same year he worked on the script for *The Amazing Dr Clitterhouse*, based on a play, in which Edward G. Robinson plays a shrink who wants to understand the criminal personality – and so joins a gang led by Bogart. It was a Robinson vehicle, but it was unusual in its sense of criminality as a trait that might be universal. Huston was not involved in the film closely (Anatole Litvak directed), but it was his first chance to observe Bogart and hear the actor speak his lines.

For another year, Bogart persevered: he played the Irish groom in *Dark Victory*, opposite Bette Davis – he got attention, but it's a stretch for his admirers to say that he was anywhere near relaxed or Bogie yet. He took the hoodlum part in *Invisible Stripes* when Raft – also in the film – announced that it was 'a Bogart role'. In Raft's estimate, the sour, ugly hoods who got killed were Bogart's territory. He had picked up the very questionable notion that the good guys in pictures – the stars – always survived. They were more than good-looking; they were virtuous, too.

Raft's opinion was not his alone. At various times, it affected Cagney and Robinson in their search for respectability. Further, by the end of the 30s, as America gradually made ready to take on a very large role of responsibility in world affairs, the favourable estimates of the gangster genre were waning.

It was at this point that Raft and Bogart were cast as

brother truckers – Joe and Paul Fabrini – in *They Drive by Night*, a film to be directed by Raoul Walsh. Raft was the evident star, with a larger part than Bogart's. Yet, in addition, he seemed to needle Bogart on set and treat him like an inferior. Walsh saw a side of Bogart that was familiar – for real or not, Bogart often appeared hungover and in a bad temper. It was common knowledge that the marriage to Mayo Methot was going badly. Bogart was worn out from complaining about bad parts.

'He disliked motion pictures,' said Walsh, 'and he disliked the hours. He'd come on set and say "What the hell are we going to do today?" He was always beefing because he had come from the stage, where he worked in the theatre at eight o'clock and at eleven he was through so that he could go out and continue his drinking. He said the salary was his only thrill.'

They Drive by Night turned out very well, but that was principally because of the presence of Ida Lupino in a supporting role. She was from England and a big theatrical family, and she was just twenty-two. In the truckers' story, she had only a supporting role – a selfish woman who has killed her husband – but it came to dominate the movie because in the courtroom, breaking into madness, Lupino gave such a startling performance. She had stolen the picture – indeed, she had served notice of a power that was never quite fulfilled. But in a way that was uncommon with actresses, she shifted the power set-up at Warners.

High Sierra was another Mark Hellinger production, and he entrusted the screenplay adaptation (from a W.R. Burnett novel) to John Huston. The omens were good: Burnett books had been filmed successfully several times already; and Huston was a hot new screenwriter. When *High Sierra* was published, in 1940, one critic could see it with Edward G. Robinson. In *The New Republic*, Max Gissen said the central character, 'Roy Earle . . . was a mixture of old-fashioned decency and sharp rebellion against the average man's role in society'. Mark those words – they are the first sighting of 'Bogie'.

The part of Earle was in fact offered to Paul Muni – and he turned it down. Next it went to George Raft who declared himself entirely out of love with the 'mad dog' element in anyone, let alone a guy who dies at the end of the picture. Meanwhile, Humphrey Bogart – no doubt encouraged by Huston and Hellinger – had sent a short, shy note to Hal Wallis, the production chief at Warners, indicating that he thought he could do Earle. The studio bought the proposal, in large part because Hellinger was anxious to give Ida Lupino the starring role, and that was a lot easier if she was playing with a studio second lead actor. You can still see the result: Ida Lupino as Marie Garson is the film's lead in the credits. Bogart earned $11,200 on the picture – and Lupino made $12,000. Raoul Walsh made $17,500, and even Huston walked off with $15,000. It was just a little picture.

* * *

High Sierra, with Ida Lupino

Lupino is very good in *High Sierra*, but Bogart is breathing new air. And at the outset of the film, a crucial revision of the script was made – to this day we are not quite sure where it came from. In the screenplay, a newspaper announces that Roy Earle has been paroled early. Then he is reunited with old criminal associates. The movie itself is very different: in the cut film, we see Earle coming out of prison. He's a slight, dark figure, with greying hair. He shuffles and he gazes up at the light, the liberty of the birds and the trees. The look of appreciation is more than anything Bogart had ever been asked to do. In the same way, he looks older and brutalized by prison. He is wounded, or wronged – not because he was ever wrongfully convicted, but because his chance has been beaten out of him.

Earle is trapped: he has been freed by a criminal conspiracy so that he can do other robberies. He is hardened – he slaps a criminal agent around and Bogart does not stifle the nastiness in Earle. But then as the story moves along, the renewed criminal life is offset by Roy's infatuation with a crippled girl, Velma (Joan Leslie), and his grudging acceptance of Marie (Lupino), though he tells her he can never love her. And beyond all that, Roy has this urge to 'break out', to be free of the whole criminal life in an existential way. The escapism may be self-destructive, finally. But in his stoical, hard-bitten response to life, Roy never succumbs to self-pity. It is as if the beefing, complaining voice that people knew in Bogart himself had taken on an edge of resigned nobility.

Something like existentialism has cut across the path of the gangster film, and if Huston and Burnett are voicing it, still Bogart gives it directness and flavour. Velma is the superficial, pleasure-loving cypher he rescues so she can turn him down. Marie is the more gloomy kindred spirit who is suited to him – and who tries to rescue him. And so *High Sierra* moves across a rural or provincial landscape, looking for a way out but essentially confined by the looming mountain-top that looks down on the petty striving of a few men and which gives a police sniper the angle that puts down the mad dog.

It was never plain sailing. At first, up in the real mountains, Bogart hated nature, the thin air and all the effort of climbing. He told Raoul Walsh that he preferred indoor pictures and lounging around. So Walsh played a game with his star. He sent him high up to that niche in the rocks where he would be shot. Then he kept him waiting in the cold and the heat that are companions in the mountains. When he trekked up to talk to Bogart, he told him the lunches had failed to arrive. The famous temper flared. Then Bogart saw it was all a joke. He laughed and maybe the first glimmerings of Earle as a beaten but endearing soul crept in on him. When Bogart and Ida Lupino began to get along, Mayo Methot appeared out of nowhere as a scowling watchdog. When you looked at Methot and Lupino, there was nothing to do but be rueful and agree that at forty with three wives Humphrey had had a fair shot.

There was no sign that the actor 'got' it yet. Not even John Huston claimed a finder's fee, though Huston had bigger plans and he may have known when to shut up. *High Sierra* was shot during the summer and fall of 1940. The Sierra was a long way away from the trouble but German troops entered Paris in June 1940 and the Battle of Britain began not long thereafter. Ida Lupino was only recently out of south London, and Bogart may have been a drunk and a sourpuss but he was no fool. He could listen and learn. Just because it's lovely up in the Sierra at that time of year why is an actor going to miss the unexpected resonance between Roy Earle's laconic fatalism and the drift of contemporary history? That's how they filmed simple little scenes like this, not too far from a love scene, the kind of thing Humphrey Bogart had never been asked to do before.

MARIE: (looking at Roy's wound): It doesn't look good, Roy. It's all red way up under your armpit. You got any fever?

ROY: I don't think so . . . Maybe I have . . . I ought to go in and see Doc.

MARIE: No, you can't do that. They might kill you. You can't trust nobody . . . not even your friends. Ten thousand dollars is a lot of money.

ROY: You ought to turn me in and live easy for the rest of your life.

MARIE: Roy . . . don't say things like that . . . even in fun!

There it is, the Bogart snarl, the willingness to put himself on a plate, like a cooked sausage, grinning at the mustard. And then the mordant gaze that watches her horror and the absolute imperturbability that refuses to soften at the sign of her loyalty, her honour, because somehow this movie is trusting us to pick up on it. This guy isn't going to beg to be liked – that's the George Raft way and it's for suckers. But not even this guy knows yet the huge affection there can be waiting for him so long as a guy doesn't ask for it.

Something else happened during the shooting of *High Sierra*. It was in the summer of 1940, under the chairmanship of Martin Dies, that the House Un-American Activities Committee made its first noises in Los Angeles. John L. Leech, allegedly an officer in the Communist Party, and an established liar, had named a few names – one of them Humphrey Bogart.

This was a disturbed time, even in Hollywood. There were committees and funds to assist Jews being persecuted in Germany, the Scottsboro boys, lettuce workers in the San Joaquin Valley – even the Screen Writers Guild. Bogart had signed on to some of those causes. He had given a little money. But the story now spread that he had been seen 'reading Karl Marx'. On 16 August, Bogart and his lawyer, Morgan Maree, met the Dies people in the Biltmore Hotel in Los Angeles. Under oath, Bogart denied his own membership of the Party. He said he had no evidence of Communist activities in the picture business. He refused to pass any opinion on whether others might be Communists. The informant was a known liar, said Bogart, and at that point he started to talk like Bogie:

I've been born an American. I've always been a loyal citizen. I have great love for my country. Anytime I would be called upon I would serve that country. I resent the intrusion and the insinuation that I am anything else . . . I think it's completely un-American [for] a man who has been, as far as I can read the papers, called a liar to be allowed to testify before a grand jury without the people accused being permitted to have an opportunity to answer those charges.

Dies backed away. He conceded that there was no evidence against Bogart. He took his committee home and the press observed that political affiliation in America was not a crime – but that insidious use of legal machinery to start a slur might be. Happy days. Six weeks later, the politically neutral Bogart made a decision: he lent his support to the presidential election (for the third time) of Franklin Roosevelt.

High Sierra isn't a great film, but it came out new in a way that was only noticed when a few local censorship organizations started saying, wait a minute, this Earle guy is pretty damn close to being sympathetic. But he's a gangster! The studio looked again, but they didn't see it yet. Earle was a killer, a thief, a loser – sure, he had a kinder side to him, and he got along in a strange tough way with Marie. But he never stopped the film and said, look, folks, I'm a reformed character. I'm a nice guy. Honest, I am. He never asked for anything. Maybe that's what Huston saw and maybe he guessed how it could fit in a new moment in American history when all of a sudden the real heroes didn't have to wear labels but could act as mean, as hard-bitten and as unsentimental as . . . Sam Spade or Rick Blaine or Philip Marlowe (or Tom Joad). Suppose you had this tight-lipped guy in a hot corner and all he did was act as if he'd been deceived – like coming to Casablanca for the waters when there were no waters anywhere near.

As war came close, there were a lot of reasons – official and semi-official – why gangsters and hoodlums should disappear from the American screen. These lurid fantasies hardly reflected well on the nation's moral character. So the studios made a pact to go gently on the outright violence of these pictures. But a shrewd commanding officer might look at Bogart and see a fellow worth having in a nasty situation. So suppose you told him to put the illegal stuff away but keep on talking as insolent and cocksure as the worst gangsters ever made. You mean, just be myself? a Bogart might have said. And that's how Huston and Hawks at least got it. And that's how Bogie came to be sour, sarcastic, lonely but sweet. Don't tell yourself the movies aren't about dreaming.

High Sierra opened in New York, on 25 January 1941, and it would prove one of Warner Brothers' best grossers of the year. In most markets (including New York and Los Angeles) they found that it did about 25 per cent over average business. The *Hollywood Reporter* said it was 'a gripping drama of great vitality and sustained suspense, as marked for its impressive characterization as its vivid action'. In the *New York Herald Tribune*, Howard Barnes wrote that 'Bogart is at once savage and sentimental; fatalistic and filled with half-formulated aspirations. His steady portrayal, even more than Raoul Walsh's staccato staging, is what makes the melodrama something more than merely exciting'. In the *New York Times*, Bosley Crowther, full of praise for Bogart, wondered if the film marked 'the twilight of the American gangster'. The actor had never had such notices before. He might have told George Raft that some deaths on screen are better than others – in *High Sierra*, he had been reunited with Pard the dog. And there was no telling the public that the happy dog had made a mistake.

Nevertheless, disputes with Raft went on. Warners reckoned to put Raft and Bogart together again as guys battling over Marlene Dietrich. That is the outline of the Raoul Walsh film, *Manpower*. But the two actors rivalled each other now in the hope that they wouldn't have to work together again. So Bogart was dropped for Edward G. Robinson who had huge and unseemly altercations with Raft.

More curious is what happened on *Out of the Fog*. This was the movie taken from Irwin Shaw's 1939 play, *The Gentle People*, a New York stage hit, with Franchot Tone as a gangster figure who terrorizes small fishermen but falls in love with the daughter of one of them (Sylvia Sidney). Then the gentle people unite against the outlaw. Initially, it was lined up as a project for Bogart and Ida Lupino, apparently on the chemistry they had shown – and felt – on *High Sierra*. At first Bogart was keen. He cabled Jack Warner: 'It seems to me that I am the logical person on the lot to play *Gentle People*. I would be greatly disappointed if I didn't get it.'

Then something went wrong. Word spread that Lupino felt she had been bullied on *High Sierra*. Bogart was perplexed. Maybe Lupino was wary of getting in deeper with Bogart, with a resentful Mayo Methot in the wings. Or maybe Lupino just felt something about the new star at Warners, John Garfield, who was only twenty-seven, and became her co-star in *Out of the Fog*. But this was probably the last disappointment Bogie would have to face at Warners, and it didn't have to last long. For something else had appeared – the stuff dreams are made of.

Dashiell Hammett's *The Maltese Falcon* was published by Knopf in 1930. Barely 200 pages, and with so much good dialogue that people automatically wondered if it might make a play, the *Falcon* was a turning point – in Hammett's career and in the establishment of a certain kind of private detective: shrewd, tough, brave, hard-boiled yet funny in his talk, and ruthlessly honest, despite the seductive enticements in the world of crime. In particular, the *Falcon* concerns a private eye – Sam

Spade – who acquires a client, a lovely woman whose name shifts like her story, and who uses Spade in an effort to secure the Maltese Falcon and who trusts that in the end his love for her will overwhelm his better instinct that she ought to be properly placed in the women's prison at Tehachapi.

Hammett himself had been a Pinkerton's operative and he knew the real dilemma as honour faced compromise in the law-enforcement business. He wrote in a very straight, hard, cold style that was itself new (or an intriguing variant on Hemingway), but in *The Maltese Falcon*, at least, he experimented with the idea of a detective who does not cave in. Spade is an original character in American fiction, and plausible. Brigid O'Shaughnessy, equally, is a character we come to place. Still, I'm not sure that the novelty and the entertainment value of the book doesn't rest in its most amiable villains – Casper Gutman and Joel Cairo, unusually talkative and florid scoundrels and page-turning engines.

The book had seven reprints in its first year and Warner Brothers bought the movie rights. A film appeared – *The Maltese Falcon* – as early as 1931. It was directed by Roy Del Ruth and it starred Ricardo Cortez as Spade and Bebe Daniels as Brigid. No one believed that the film had done justice to the book, and so a second version of the story appeared in 1936 – *Satan Met a Lady*, directed by William Dieterle, and with Warren William and Bette Davis. This version was less faithful to the novel and even more astray.

One man at least was amazed by this lapse in Hollywood common sense: John Huston admired the novel
above all because it seemed to have been written for the
screen. Yards of it, he said, could simply be retyped as a
film script instead of a novel. Anyone thinking that that
was a modest deflection of proper praise should look at
the book and the third picture. It isn't just that Huston
got it right – he simply filmed it accurately. He let it
work. He saw that it was a comi-tragic bridge game, a
no-holds-barred four-hander. And he guessed that
Spade and Bogart were like twins lost at birth and desperate to be reunited.

Of course, Huston was the more excited or focused
on the work in that it was the culmination of a long-
held plan in which he would be promoted to the position of writer-director. Perhaps more than on any film
he would ever make, Huston had a storyboard of
sketches. He had been over this with his friend, the
director William Wyler, and the picture's producer,
Henry Blanke. He was in a position of such secure confidence with the material that he could devote all his
energy to the filming itself, and the playing. But as with
so many Warner Brothers projects, he had to find a way
around that stubborn impediment, George Raft.

The studio wisdom held that Raft was an obvious
Sam Spade – and Raft had played in Hammett already
in the 1935 film of *The Glass Key*. At a stretch, Raft could
have been the impassive private eye dancing his way
through the intrigue. But he could not have delivered

the rueful amusement waiting in Bogart's eyes, and he did not have it in him to be savagely in love with Brigid O'Shaughnessy. For Huston's concept of the tough loner who barely survives intact, that vulnerability was essential and it was what Huston had seen and helped to flower in *High Sierra*.

What was Raft holding out for? Did he want to play Emile Zola or Vincent Van Gogh? The studio gave him *The Maltese Falcon* to read, and sure enough, he came back with 'this is not an important picture', and the reminder to Jack Warner himself that George had been promised important pictures. He may well have added that he was nervous about lending himself to a first-time director. There are as many reasons for turning a part down as there are for taking it, and in the end the reasons are froth in the wind next to that instinct that could be carried on a look between Bogart and Huston without needing to know there would be six pictures, an Oscar, a friendship and a eulogy where the one man could speak of pride at seeing such courage in the wreck who went up and downstairs in the dumb waiter because he wasn't strong enough to manage the stairs.

Huston knew something? No, if you had asked him then in 1941 he'd have said it was just a guess, a gambler's guess. But Huston's intuition and his way of seeing had worked on *High Sierra* and how he cast Roy Earle back before prison and the bad luck to a time when Earle believed in himself. In *The Maltese Falcon*, there is a good deal of cinematography of Bogart in

With Peter Lorre, *The Maltese Falcon*

full figure, just strolling around, crossing through space, leaving the room. These are mundane movements, but they are like music for the man's song. He begins to expand. It is the first film that guessed or half understood, just get Bogie walking and we're with him. On his side. And as Huston said, years later, 'Bogie was a medium-sized man, not particularly impressive – until the right part. Those lights and shadows composed themselves into another, nobler personality: heroic, as in *High Sierra*. I swear the camera has a way of looking into a person and perceiving things that the naked eye doesn't register.'

The key role of Brigid was being dangled in front of Mary Astor and Geraldine Fitzgerald – so it's worth noting that Astor was the older of the two by six years. Astor had many attributes of the lady – she was classy in her looks and she was better educated than many actresses. In Europe, the Astors were a noble family. But she had had several affairs and marriages, not least a notorious liaison with the writer George S. Kaufman from which her sexual diary – uncommonly candid – had been used against her in court. She had married again, and she had just had a child, so she was especially happy. But she loved the script – she called it a humdinger; she took to Huston quickly (it is known that they had an affair during the shooting of the sort that begins in private coaching); and she said in her autobiography that Bogart was an old friend, too.

What Mary Astor liked about the part was that this

woman changed her story and her name as if changing her hat. And her maturity is important to the film. A kid would have been more naturally seductive, but the older woman makes her fit company for the foursome – these are all hardened types. So Astor, like Bogart, would benefit enormously from the presence of two people who were both of them fairly new to American film. Peter Lorre – Huston's Joel Cairo – was very experienced in German theatre and as the murderer in Fritz Lang's *M*. He had had several years in America, a lot of Mr Moto films and some worthy literary pictures – he had done Raskolnikov for Sternberg in *Crime and Punishment*. But he was an oddity and it's fair to say that Huston noticed his eccentric genius and gave it an unusual opening.

Even when the book first appeared, Hammett had been chided by Knopf for its flagrant if icy homosexuality, and this really hinges on the characters of Cairo, Gutman and Wilma, the gunsel. Huston was fascinated by Lorre and saw that he was worthy of being a lead, or one in a quartet of supporting actors.

But the triumph of this approach was to see that Gutman – the lazily eloquent criminal master-mind, fencing with Spade in so much cross-talk – could be Sydney Greenstreet, a successful English stage actor, sixty already, who had never made a film before. He was large, silky, epicene and a connoisseur of intricacy and wickedness – or so it seemed. In fact, he had not always been a villain on the stage. He had made a modest career out of playing with Alfred Lunt and Lynn Fontanne, and Huston saw him for the first time acting with them in Robert Sherwood's *There Shall Be No Night*. Huston had a hunch and he was right – Greenstreet proved to be the surprise hit of the movie and the person audiences most enjoyed. *The Maltese Falcon* was one key step in the shift in Bogart from hoodlum to hero, but it was the picture that gave Greenstreet ten years and a kind of immortality on screen. But the more this fat man talked, the more philosophy emerged in Bogart's taciturn responses.

For the first time in his career, Bogart was talking to intelligent, devious characters. Indeed, Gutman declares himself at the start: he is fat from eloquence, not evil – 'I distrust a close-mouthed man. He generally picks the wrong time to talk and says the wrong things. Talking's something you can't do judiciously unless you keep in practice. We'll get along, sir, that we will.' And so it turns out. Spade wins the case (if you like), but Gutman goes free – and wonders if Spade won't accompany him and Cairo to Constantinople in onward pursuit of the falcon. It's a mystery that in times of penury and writers' block, Hammett didn't let his fondness for those three companions in talk inspire further novels.

The articulate villain is about to be born in American films – sometimes he is fat, sometimes thin; sometimes swish , sometimes epigrammatic. It is a small, enviable school that includes Waldo Lydecker (Clifton Webb) in *Laura*; Addison de Witt (George Sanders) in *All About*

Eve; Joe Gillis (William Holden) in *Sunset Blvd* – talking long after he's dead; Uncle Lon (Louis Calhern) in *The Asphalt Jungle*; Robert Ryan in *Crossfire*; or Bruno Anthony (Robert Walker) in *Strangers on a Train*. The better these men talk the more necessary it is not to trust them – and at the end of the line sits their ultimate monster, Noah Cross in *Chinatown*, embodied by an ancient John Huston, as wrinkled as a lizard. I don't think it's going too far to say that in art and in life Huston had practised this dangerous, yarn-spinning tone until it became him.

And Bogart. For as *The Maltese Falcon* spins on, and then later as we exult in the two films by Howard Hawks, what we notice above all is that the power of speech has descended on Bogart and rescued him from moroseness. This shows in the close-to-comic routines with Cairo and Gutman, but above all it's in the relationship with Brigid that Spade's terrible eloquence begins. In all their early meetings, she is the talker, playing with names, moods and tones until she has him. But then, at the close of the book – and only in modestly reduced form in the film – he lets her have it. And there's nothing less than moral anger in Bogart's performances, a hatred of her that extends to his own weakness:

Spade pulled his hand out of hers. He no longer either smiled or grimaced. His wet yellow face was set hard and deeply lined. His eyes burned madly. He said: 'Listen. This isn't a damned bit of good. You'll never understand me, but I'll try once more and then we'll give it up. Listen. When a man's partner is killed he's supposed to do something about it. It doesn't make any difference what you thought of him. He was your partner and you're supposed to do something about it. Then it happens we were in the detective business. Well, when one of your organization gets killed it's bad business to let the killer get away with it. It's bad all around – bad for that one organization, bad for every detective everywhere. Third, I'm a detective and expecting me to run criminals down and then let them go free is like asking a dog to catch a rabbit and let it go. It can be done, all right, and sometimes it is done, but it's not the natural thing. The only way I would have let you go was by letting Gutman and Cairo and the kid go. That's –'

'You're not serious,' she said. 'You don't expect me to think that those things you're saying are sufficient reason for sending me to the '

'Wait till I'm through and then you can talk. Fourth, no matter what I wanted to do now it would be absolutely impossible for me to let you go without having myself dragged to the gallows with the others. Next, I've no reason in god's world to think I can trust you and if I did this and got away with it you'd have something on me that you could use whenever you happened to want to. That's five of them. The sixth would be that, since I've got something on you, I couldn't be sure you wouldn't decide to shoot a hole in me some day. Seventh, I don't even like the idea of thinking that there might be one chance in a hundred that you'd played me for a sucker. And eighth but that's enough. All those on one side. Maybe some of them are unimportant. I won't argue about that. But look at the number of them. Now on the other side you've got what? All we've got is the fact that maybe you love me and maybe I love you.'

'You know,' she whispered, 'whether you do or not.'

'I don't. It's easy enough to be nuts about you.' He looked hungrily from her hair to her feet and up to her eyes again. 'But I don't know what that amounts to. Does anybody ever? [think of the hill of beans speech to come] But suppose I do? What of it? Maybe next month I won't. I've been through before – when it lasted that long. Then what? Then I'll think I played the sap. And if I did it and got sent over then I'd be sure I was the sap. Hell, if I send you over I'll be as sorry as hell – I'll have some rotten nights – but that'll be all. Listen.' He took her by the shoulders and bent her back, leaning over her. 'If that doesn't mean anything to you forget it and we'll make it this: I won't because all of me wants to – and because – God damn you – you've counted on that with me the same as you counted on that with the others.' He took his hands from her shoulders and let them fall to his sides.

This is template stuff: it's the basis for the slightly sadistic, skin-crawling attraction between the sexes in everyone from Cornell Woolrich to James M. Cain and Jim Thompson. It's the rhetoric of film noir, and you can argue that it works because of a rooted fear and loathing for women in the tough male point of view. It's intriguing to wonder how far Huston had noticed a sarcasm that Bogart ached to release on Mayo Methot. As Huston saw it, when the couple fought, the wife threw things at Bogie. So he seldom got a word in. Now, Huston his pal, had found the battered cry of the wounded lover. The world was on the way to getting at this private feeling in Bogart – the gloomy certainty that he was not appreciated. So Spade's integrity is very close to Bogart's dream of being someone worthwhile.

On the first scenes shot, the studio felt that Bogart's timing was too slow. They urged Huston to hurry him up, and the director said he would do so. In fact, it's not clear what happened. No one had that much experience of Bogart taking advice. Huston was encouraging a close comradeship on set. He took the unit over to the Lakeside Golf Club for lunch. He laid on drinks for everyone – far from the standard factory method – and he encouraged rehearsal and improvisation before any scene was shot. Above all, Huston sought from the players their natural rhythms. Sydney Greenstreet had been very nervous before he began, and he asked Mary Astor for help. But Huston made it clear that he cherished the actor's serpentine delivery and his delight at being listened to.

The day came when Bogart and Astor kissed for the camera – after ten years it was the first Bogart kiss that audiences were meant to soak up and be a part of. He did his best, but he had a problem. Saliva seemed to gather in his mouth. Was it something to do with that lip? They tried several takes, but the problem persisted.

Astor did all she could to be encouraging and at last they got it OK.

All of a sudden, at Warners, George Raft became known as a fall guy or a stooge as people rejoiced in Bogart's effortless and fluent performance. The picture had come in way under budget, thanks to Huston's preparations. Not everyone recognized quite how novel a venture it was, but anyone could feel the entertainment value. Grant that Greenstreet and Lorre would do another seven films at Warners as a team, and you can see how much of a model picture the Hammett had proved. The reviews were very good, with special praise going to Huston, Greenstreet, Astor and Bogart. The film made money and when the Oscar nominations were released, there it was as one of ten films up for Best Picture. Huston picked up a nod for best screenplay and Sydney Greenstreet won the supporting actor Oscar at his first attempt. Bogart was not nominated, but that made no difference to the way in which his prospects were now transformed. He could hold his head up, and that was all he had ever required.

So the studio rewrote its own script: persuaded that Bogart could play the lead in a picture, they elected to tear up his old contract and re-negotiate with his agent, Sam Jaffe. Jaffe was not a front-rank operator, but he was good and dogged; he loved Bogart, and the actor trusted him. Their business relationship worked out well, but it was a measure of Bogart's wish for loyalty.

All along, Bogart had reckoned that the studio would see sense. Now they treated him better: there was more vacation, time for freelance radio jobs and his weekly take went up from $1,750 to $2,750. The word went around that Bogart had made it. Jack Warner declared that he was one of the best talents they had. But still the new deal was just a stepping-stone, and the breakthrough had depended on the panache and the unique team spirit on a John Huston picture.

For a moment, Bogart marked time. He was assigned to *All Through the Night* in which he played Gloves Donohue, an ex-gangster who has turned to gambling as the war opens. He discovers a plot by Conrad Veidt (with Peter Lorre and Judith Anderson as sidekicks) to blow up a ship in New York harbour and sets out to defeat the Nazis. It's an uneasy film in which an ironic regard for sabotage turns serious (it appeared just after Pearl Harbor), and in which a few comics – William Demarest, Phil Silvers and Jackie Gleason – compete for screen time.

That was followed by *The Big Shot*, the last of his B pictures, and a shameless throwback to the 1930s. He played a three-time loser in a prison-break story in an undistinguished film made by a second-rate cast and directed by Lewis Seiler. What came next was *Across the Pacific*, John Huston's second film, though written by someone else, Richard Macaulay. Set in Panama, it posed Bogart against spies again. The cast included Sydney Greenstreet and Mary Astor and it was equally

Casablanca, Rick and Ilsa

evident as part of that studio's dumb wish, after *The Maltese Falcon*, that this Hammett guy had other stories available. It's nowhere near the quality of the first film, in part perhaps because the insouciant Huston simply took off two-thirds of the way through and accepted a commission in the Army. He was for the real thing, but as a joke he left Bogart behind in a rare, suspenseful predicament that the rest of the film had to sort out. It had been a Huston joke – but Bogart was less adventurous or whimsical, and he saw it as a measure of his friend's irresponsibility. So the war and war movies had knocked Bogie around a bit, enough to leave him wary about what might be coming next.

'Here's looking at you,' Rick will say to Ilsa, and it's not a bad explanation of the whole thing. For as Bogart also recalled, he had been doing movies, of a kind, for twenty years. In all that time, no one had thought too much of him, and no one had dared think that he had sex appeal on screen. Now, in the wake of this thing called *Casablanca*, people were declaring that he had sex appeal. 'The thing is,' announced Bogart, 'if Ingrid stopped to look at you, you'd got sex appeal!' After all, you couldn't do sex on screen, but you could look at people. And it was enough.

Yes, it was a play first, *Everyone Comes to Rick's*, but nobody had seen the work in performance. So it amounted to a Hollywood measure of good fortune that an unknown play could become a classic. It was a part of this magic, no doubt, that had the play and the authors' letter of submission arrive at Warner Brothers' Burbank studio the day after Pearl Harbor. Not that crazy luck ever abated: for the Allied forces occupied Casablanca in Morocco just as the film came ready to be opened. Whereupon the hardened warriors of the movie looked up in amazement to hear that there might be a real Casablanca – so far from Burbank – where hostilities could be entered into.

The story is told, with daft pride, of how *Casablanca* was lucky it got made, of how the casting could have been so different, of how it might have been not just George Raft, but even Ronald Reagan as Rick. Why, if Reagan had had that part, you can surmise, there would have been no need for him to be president, too. In fact, *Casablanca* went from idea to finished picture with due speed and decisiveness. What that means is that, at a certain moment, the studio would consider everyone it had on board who was remotely suited to a role. You do that to be prepared in the event of any scheduling problems – because you know, above all, that you cannot delay the enterprise.

I think it is far more accurate to what happened to say that the best people available made *Casablanca*, and made it so well that its enormous hokiness can still slip past so some feel they have seen a war movie instead of a great romance. So allow that the picture was made – in the sense of conceived and executed – by Hal Wallis (who was at that time probably the best motion picture executive around) and Michael Curtiz, Hungarian-born, but an ideal director of romantic, slightly tongue-in-cheek material.

And those two men knew from early on that *Casablanca* had to be a Bogart picture. Its suspense needed his courage and resolve. Its love story needed the extent to which he could be scarred by a woman – that feeling left at the end of *The Maltese Falcon* that in sending Brigid to prison, or worse, Sam is never going to be the same again. And it needed the just and plausible notion that his intrinsic, well-guarded solitude, his independence, would break down and join the united cause. In short, Bogart's rueful gaze and his weary voice were a proper task force to face fascism and to discard neutrality and self-concern.

For under the Burbank lights a weird United Nations was being formed. It was only surface deep, like the scar that proved Victor Laszlo had been in a concentration camp. But it was a mood fundamental to the heady innocence of the years 1943–5. In a way, acting should not have meant so much just then – for it was so removed from the terrible wartime reality. But Bogart's strength and charm is directly connected to America's failure to perceive its own ignorance or irrelevance at this moment of crisis and dawning empire.

The most important thing to stress is that so much of the movie existed in the play, by Murray Burnett and Joan Alison – Rick, his café, Casablanca, the pattern of Vichy and Gestapo, the letters of transit hidden in Sam's piano, Sam, 'As Time Goes By', a mistress from the past. It is only with that woman that the play and the movie begin to diverge. In the play, the woman was an American, named Lois Meredith – which may account for the early guess, from Hal Wallis, that *Casablanca* would be made with Bogart and Ann Sheridan.

The closest study of the film (by Aljean Harmetz in her excellent and very fair book, *Round Up the Usual Suspects*), cannot be clear on the scripting process. And people who were part of it at the time have offered histories which they later corrected. You can say that that is the urge to claim credit on a big hit, but it is also a just reflection of the intricate and overlapping ways in which screenplays were written in Hollywood in the golden age. Very often, it was hard to recollect who did what when in a world where people were sometimes working behind others' backs. It is creative, but it can be espionage, too. For the purpose of this short study, one thing is plain in hindsight just as it must have made for clarity in the writing: the several writers took it for granted that Rick was going to be Bogart. That means that they aspired to finding lines worthy of his bleak, needling voice and those hopeless but yearning eyes. Meanwhile, all Bogart had to do was preserve his cynicism and his dismay as nearly everything in his life got better. I say 'nearly', because Mayo was still his noisy companion. Nobody's perfect?

Wallis showed the play to several writers. One of them, Robert Buckner (he had worked on *Jezebel* and

Yankee Doodle Dandy), told the boss, 'I don't believe the story or the characters. Its main situations and the basic relations of the principals are completely censorable and messy, its big moment is sheer hokum melodrama of the E. Phillips Oppenheim variety; and this guy Rick is two-parts Hemingway, one part Scott Fitzgerald, and a dash of café Christ.'

Hold on to that – it helps sustain the notion that there were some smart people in Hollywood, even if it reminds us all to appreciate the virtue of what another writer would call 'slick shit'. You could easily say that Buckner's crushing verdict was on the money – as well as a promise of more money. The magic in people like Hal Wallis was how to grasp such contradictions.

The project was given to a team – Wally Kline and Aeneas Mackenzie – but their work was never referred to again. At that point, as if he had been gathering points of reference, Wallis assigned the script to Philip and Julius Epstein, twin brothers, sardonic wits and the best in the business. They had done *Four Daughters*, *Four Wives* and *Strawberry Blonde*, and at that time, despite their tough manner, they were known for love stories. They wrote together, and they made good progress, but they had another obligation – to John Huston – to help on one of his military documentaries. It seems to have been to cover that hiatus that Wallis also put Howard Koch on the picture – separately, as they say. Koch was a match for the Epsteins: trained by Orson Welles at the Mercury Theatre, he had written *Sergeant York* and *The*

Letter (an outstanding piece of construction). Better still, he had authentic leftist views for a story that – in Wallis's eyes – was always about a neutral coming to the aid of a just cause.

No one knows the exact pattern of work now. Koch did once claim full credit, but he then made a very decent correction (explained by faulty memory) when the Epsteins explained that it was their drafts Howard had been doctoring. They knew because they'd been rewriting his stuff! Above all, I think that one has to appreciate the work of Hal Wallis, presiding over these writers – and others – improving the script until the movie works like clockwork or slick shit.

In the event, the credits – and the plaque on the screenplay Oscar – say the Epsteins and Howard Koch, and all three deserved their piece of it. But then remember this. Casey Robinson (he had written *Dark Victory* and *All This and Heaven, Too*) said he stumbled on the play one day and recommended it to Wallis. Casey was then in a love affair with the Russian dancer Tamara Toumanova – so he told Wallis, make the girl foreign.

Time passes. The film is being shot, with Bogart and Ingrid Bergman, but Bogart was walking off the set one day because he said the love story was shit – and not even the slick kind. So Robinson was hired on to rewrite day by day to give the love story a bit more class. And it was Robinson who said – above it all – that Wallis wrote stuff himself. For instance, he did the last line – 'Louis, I think this is the start of a beautiful friendship.' Today, that shameless get-off line speaks to the lasting bonds of affection between golden-age Hollywood and ourselves – the tarnished coinage of movies. If you'd been there and you thought of a sweet line they might have used it. So what do you want now – $50 or the memory? Like 'Play it again, Sam.' Everyone remembers that line, though it isn't in the picture.

And lines like that are *Casablanca* – and in great films of its era. If you could prove beyond a doubt that you wrote five great lines from *Casablanca* – hill of beans, the waters, the last line, here's looking at you kid, and play it, you're home, in the pantheon. All Hal Wallis did was pick the best lines and put them in order, and dream up Bergman and Bogart – she like a great flower waiting to be inhaled, and he not wanting to remember how to sniff. She's so open and he's so guarded. And in the end maybe it was because he was chronically shy with women. I kissed him, said Bergman, but I never knew him.

Once the idea of making the girl foreign had settled, there was a brief lull – after all, everyone in Hollywood liked to survey the available talent. The French actress Michèle Morgan was considered. She was only twenty-two. She had done *Quai des Brumes* in Paris and *Joan of Paris* in Los Angeles. She was a beauty but pretty cool – and then Wallis hit the roof when he heard she was asking for $55,000. He looked at Edwige Feuillère and Hedy Lamarr – he said the picture was going to be like *Pepe le Moko*. But already Wallis was talking to David

O. Selznick who had Ingrid Bergman under contract. These were early days in her career. She had not had an American hit yet. But anyone who met her was crazy for her. She could act. She had real character or power – no one was going to stop looking at her because she was with Bogart. As for Bogie, his reaction is not clear. He and Ingrid were not close, and somehow that helped in the suggestion that Rick was struggling to forget her. And you could believe that until you caught the first dark look when he sees her again, when self-pity, anger and revenge are all there, waiting to see which is capable of murder. Rick isn't just carrying a torch for Ilsa. He's been left crazy by her. It's in letting her go the second time that he shakes off that self-pity and becomes sane again. But one of Bogart's great achievements was in persuading us of the lingering, wounded imprint of the past and a man's inability to forget.

Once Warners had got *Casablanca* in the can, they knew the kind of trick and commodity it was. That's why they tried to remake it over the next several years – because they never respected chance or magic. But recipes based on the same old ingredients never cohered in the same way. Except for *To Have and Have Not* – and there something else has happened: one trusted genre has been given up for another. It may be true that Bogart and Bergman were fretting over the lack of an ending. Hal Wallis simply trusted that someone would find a plot resolution and an exit line – looking like the stagiest moment in the film – that would live in history and which could beg to be accepted as a gloss on that immense, hideous and ultimately uncontainable thing: the Second World War. *Casablanca* had the trick required of contemporary war movies: take the damn thing seriously, but say it's going to be all right. I think that's what Julius Epstein meant by 'slick shit' – a very tidy, friction-free way of dealing with bad stuff. Truth to tell, it is a very workable title for a history of Hollywood.

Consider this summation of the war and its problems: Ugarte is shot and killed, but that is what Peter Lorre was for in these times – he was a colourful fall guy. What he got out of it was steady work and the day-by-day illusion of being one of Bogart's friends. Bogie liked the little guy, teased him and needled him, and exchanged worldly philosophy with him. Strasser gets killed. And, naturally, Strasser deserved it. He was the epitome of the Gestapo. Apart from that? Well, Ilsa and Victor get away. Rick and Louis are headed for the interior. Every other story in *Casablanca* ends kindly in the spirit that allows the croupier (Marcel Dalio) to bring up a winning number at roulette so that the young lovers won't be compromised. Sam presides at the piano like an icon for liberal thinking. A fabulous air of team spirit hangs over the café scenes – like tobacco smoke that has no risks. Wouldn't it be pretty to think that things were just so?

The previews were successful. The trailers were made. And in time the Allied war effort gave *Casablanca* a friendly nod of appreciation and a way of overcoming one last studio worry – did enough people know where Casablanca was? As a part of the marketing effort, the studio put out several stories to say that the Bogie-man was no more. Villainy had yielded to romance and duty. Humphrey Bogart was a reformed character. Of course, he was the same as ever. It was just that the world had found a way to make him palatable – like learning to eat oysters.

The picture opened, and in time the numbers worked out as follows: on a cost of $1.03 million, the film had rentals of $3.015 million. By 1955, the revenue to the studio from the picture was $6.8 million. Grant that it plays still, on DVD and any other form that has come along, and the film has likely doubled that income figure – all without a penny of the profits contracted out in residuals. The way it was meant to be in Hollywood. You do not have to rely on the numbers. Over sixty years later, you know the picture and its raffish atmosphere.

Casablanca won Best Picture and there was a famous confusion as both Jack Warner and Hal Wallis stood up to collect the Oscar. Warner raced to the stage and the bond between the two men was over – the way Hollywood really is. In 1944, Wallis quit Warners and set up his own unit at Paramount. In winning Best Picture, *Casablanca* didn't exactly conquer the world. The competition was not high: *For Whom the Bell Tolls*; *Heaven Can Wait*; *The Human Comedy*; *In Which We Serve*; *Madame Curie*; *The More the Merrier*; *The Ox-Bow Incident*; *The Song of Bernadette*; *Watch on the Rhine*.

Michael Curtiz won as best director. Bogart was nominated but lost to Paul Lukas in *Watch on the Rhine*. Ingrid was nominated, but for her Spanish peasant in *For Whom the Bell Tolls* – she lost to Jennifer Jones as *Bernadette*. Claude Rains lost supporting actor to Charles Coburn in *The More the Merrier*. *Casablanca* lost for photography, score and editing, too. Of course, in any year now, it's fact that *Casablanca* plays more times than all the other 1943 nominees put together. In his white tuxedo jacket, with a new toupee, crisp and boyish (made for him by Venetia Peterson – a girlfriend, on and off, and good value because her toupee looked smashing in the mirror), or in a trench coat and a fedora, with the shadow of the hat brim leaving his eyes just visible, Bogie was the spirit of alliance and foreboding optimism. He was one of us. So we became a little like him.

Just as everyone had been in two or three minds over *Casablanca* as it was made, so they all agreed once they saw it. The magic with which the Allies had occupied north Africa for the film's opening was lost on no one – and Warners rejoiced that suddenly all the idiots knew where the damned place was. It managed to seem part of the war effort to be hip to the picture, and all over the land the fantasy passed into instant legend: thus the cockamamie film was really true to America. If you are interested in mass delusion handled without discomfort, this may be the height of Hollywood. Just a few years later, the Marx Brothers proposed to film *A Night in Casablanca*. We think not, said Warner Brothers – we own the right to the place. At which Groucho retorted that they might as well try the scam that they owned 'Brothers', too.

And Bogie went to Casablanca – the ghost in the real place. It's not too hard to believe that the real Bogart was sometimes irked at being hailed as Rick. But like many Hollywood successes, he had the occasional yearning to serve. So he declared that he would give up his four-week vacation to go on a tour of bases. Where better to start than in Casablanca? The party was four: Bogie and Mayo Methot, with another actor, Don Cummings, and an accordion-player, Ralph Hark. Hark played while Mayo sang torch songs, and Bogie and Cummings did half-improvised skits. The reports are not encouraging, and tend to make Bob Hope's show feel like the Ziegfeld Follies (Hope, don't forget, was probably the most popular star of the moment, not least because he could remember 75 per cent of the largest treasure house of jokes known to man).

The experience could be testing. Bogie and his wife got drunk, and they did not honestly enjoy the rigours of camp life. They were seriously together, and unhappily not much in love. At one point, they were shipped into Naples and told to perform, at the San Carlo Opera House. It held 3,500 exhausted troops, and when Bogart came on (the witness is cartoonist Bill Mauldin) and went into a gangster routine, 'Hey, I'm forming a mob to go back to the States – any of you guys want to come with me?', the bleak truth of their situation was too much. The guys were silent, dazzled by celebrity but horrified by the trite invitation. All of a sudden, Bogart felt lost, and he never forgot the hush and the pathos in that packed theatre. Of course, he had given up the stage years earlier. There were moments when the famous actor was happy to withdraw and let Mayo sing a song – even if the troops hardly knew who she was.

It was in southern Italy that Bogart was reunited with Captain John Huston of the Army Signal Corps. They caroused and it was when drunk that Mayo tried to sing 'More Than You Know', and could hardly finish the number – to Huston's evident contempt (the scene is referred to in the later film, *Key Largo*). Bogart got drunk too and one night he had the nerve to tell a general to fuck off when the officer had asked for a little peace and quiet. One way or another, the tour was stopped short – Bogart had to be back in Hollywood by January 1944 to keep a date with Howard Hawks and *To Have and Have Not*.

To Have and Have Not was from a novel by Ernest Hemingway, whose reputation stood very high. A major movie event in the background was the filming of *For Whom the Bell Tolls* in the Californian Sierra. Gary Cooper was the Hemingway hero again – he had been the young soldier in *A Farewell to Arms*, too. And the role of the Spanish partisan who becomes his lover had gone to

Ingrid Bergman, after the first choice – dancer Vera Zorina – had proved inadequate in the part. *To Have and Have Not* would mark Bogart's most significant liaison with a real artist – but the artist was not Hemingway. It was Howard Hawks, the instigator of the project, and the auteur in that he intended it to be all about him.

In January 1944, Howard Hawks was forty-seven, tall, grey-haired, an elegant dandy, a sportsman, a dreamer and a womanizer. As seen from the outside, he could seem austere, forbidding, too perfect to be true. The inside revealed the accuracy of that impression: he was a liar, a fantasist, a gambler and as cold as ice. The judge of that was his second wife, Nancy 'Slim' Gross, for whom he had abandoned a prior wife, Athole Shearer (the sister of Norma and sister-in-law to Irving Thalberg), and three children (one of them adopted). 'Abandoned' might seem a harsh word, but Hawks had moved on from one wife (mentally unstable) to another, much younger, very beautiful and the height of fashion.

At the same time, Hawks was a very successful professional director, especially adept at dealing with men in action and their romances: he had made *Scarface*, *The Crowd Roars*, *Twentieth Century*, *Ceiling Zero*, *Bringing Up Baby*, *Only Angels Have Wings* and *Sergeant York*. But it was in the years of his marriage to Nancy (1941–8), that he would do his greatest work: *His Girl Friday*, *To Have and Have Not*, *The Big Sleep*, *Red River*. He adored Nancy and her looks. He was, shall we say, 'happy' – it is a nebulous or fickle state in Hollywood – but his success had only made him the more ardent a womanizer. Just looking, he thought, kept you free.

This is how the story goes. One day, Howard and Nancy were in their beautiful Brentwood home. As was her wont, Nancy was leafing through magazines. She was going through the latest issue of *Harper's Bazaar* when she noticed this picture – of a young woman in elegant clothes outside the door of an American Red Cross Service office – the Blood Donor bureau. The woman had the look of a femme fatale from a film noir or, granted this location, a thirsty vampire eager for a drink. It was a fashion picture (the clothes she wore were upmarket) but the use of a war setting exactly reflected the hip attitude to the war – the *Casablanca* spirit.

Nancy passed the magazine over to Howard with a 'What do you think of her?'

It may be that she soon regretted her generosity, but she was the fond, junior wife of a great movie director and she understood how far he depended on visual stimulation. She was struck by the insolent look in the young woman's face. Howard? Well, let's just say he was struck. He put his people on the research job and it didn't take long to discover that the model was Betty Joan Perske, from the Bronx, aged eighteen. That was the real name, but at the age of eight she picked up another family name – Betty Bacal – less Jewish? More American? In time, a second 'l' would slip in, with a

Hollywood first name 'Lauren'. There's genius in that name, as well as transformation or self-invention. She had attended the American Academy of Dramatic Art and done a few small things on Broadway. The eighteen was hard to credit with those knowing eyes, the deep voice and the ability to find a name like 'Lauren Bacall'. But war does encourage precocity. Sometimes the glory-seekers have to grow up in a hurry.

Through the agency of his friend, Charlie Feldman, Hawks invited Ms Perske to come out to Los Angeles. She'd get a round-trip train fare, a modest hotel and $50 a week until she shot her test. Everything would depend on that. She had benefit of make-up men, hairdressers and dental authorities. She mixed with writers and actors and she met Hawks and Nancy. She was socializing and being brought along. She realized that her boss's wife was only a few years her senior. Who knows what the real 'Slim' realized. The test was a hit. The studio, Warner Brothers, liked it. And Lauren Bacall signed a personal service contract with Howard Hawks starting at $100 a week, and rising thereafter.

Alchemy was under way, yet Bogart knew nothing about it. Hawks was the wizard and the sultan, testing Bacall's voice, giving her exercises to deepen it, and conspiring with writers like Jules Furthman and William Faulkner over things she could say on screen that were so provocative you didn't know whether to laugh or fall in love. Bacall's own book about this time – *By Myself* – says nothing about Hawks doing anything more than

re-creating her, though she admits that she realized
Hawks had a deep need to discover and create some
screen phenomenon, a woman who was so sexy she
teased every man who looked at her. *By Myself* refers to
no romantic life for the young actress in those heady
days of 1943. Take it or leave it.

That's what Bacall had to do when Hawks said that
he was thinking of putting her in *To Have and Have Not*.
Bacall never mentions reading that novel (though it was
in print) – better not to when the reading would reveal
that it had no part for her. In the book Harry Morgan is
a tough, hard-luck skipper with a wife, Marie, middle-
aged, coarse, loving, but with no more glamour than a
tin of fishing bait. The novel is the most political Hemingway ever wrote; it is tough and down-to-earth and
free from sentimentality; and it is the only novel he
wrote that had a toehold in the real America. It ends
badly, as you know it must. Harry is a goner. Magic
never gets a look in. It might make a good, tough, sour
film. But not the one Hawks had in mind.

Hawks told her it might be Bogart or Cary Grant
playing opposite her – she crossed her fingers for Grant.
But then one day, with Hawks, she dropped in on the
set of *Passage to Marseilles*, shooting at Warners, with
Bogart and Michèle Morgan. It was their first meeting.
'There was no clap of thunder,' she would write. 'Bogart was slighter than I imagined – five feet ten and a half
[he was actually two inches shorter], wearing his costume of no-shape trousers, cotton shirt and scarf

around his neck. Nothing of import was said – we didn't stay long – but he seemed a friendly man.'

She rehearsed scenes with John Ridgely, love scenes with Hawks correcting them, but they were meant for Bogart and they were based on the principle of using *To Have and Have Not* to put the standard Bogart figure to the test of some superb, inexplicable infant sexpot who was more insolent than he was, but who used the insolence for a mask to hide her total, uncritical love. The wisdom of the set-up – why not call it genius, for it's where Hawks' creativity lay – was to combine a sensational debut with the perfect display case for the new Bogart: it was Rick, with extra wit and a knock-out dame who might have to be restrained from fellating him. Every fantasy was catered, too – not least Howard's, who saw himself picking up the breathlessly available actress after every day's work. But magic is an imp with its own caprice: the movie 'Slim' fell for the wreck with a toupee and a marital problem at home. And all under the vague but sultry smoke of Ernest Hemingway being remade as screwball romance.

Did they fall in love with each other, or with the astonishing seductiveness of the film world Hawks was making for them? *To Have and Have Not* was billed as Hemingwayesque and as a war film, but in truth it's a love story in which the veteran star meets the ingénue he was not smart enough to dream up himself. Is it really such a surprise that two creatures of the movie age should actually fall in love? And if they were falling

Steve and Slim, *To Have and Have Not*

who were they to make the exact map of it all at the same time? It was too big for them to argue with: there are no real-life love stories on a film set bigger than this – no more reckless proofs of movie magic. The meeting made the film a sensation just as much as the debut of Bacall or Bogart's first chance to live out a romantic dream. He had never been so happy before, so sublime, with the piano doodling of Hoagy Carmichael and the swagger of this sexy girl, tottering off into a blissful future that would end the instant their movie stopped.

Of course, life might not be as easy. They would not have Jules Furthman to write their lines, or Sid Hickox to light them, let alone Hawks to polish the whole thing. Bacall was smart enough to observe – maybe she was smarter than Bogart: 'Howard had a brilliantly creative work method,' she noted. 'Each morning when we got to the set, he, Bogie and I and whoever else might be in the scene, and the script girl would sit in a circle in canvas chairs with our names on them and read the scene. Almost unfailingly Howard would bring in additional dialogue for the scenes of sex and innuendo between Bogie and me. After we'd gone over the words several times and changed whatever Bogie or Howard thought should be changed, Howard would ask an electrician for a work light – one light on the set – and we'd go through the scene on the set to see how it felt. Howard said, 'Move around – see where it feels most comfortable.' Only after all that had been worked out did he call Sid Hickox and talk about camera set-ups. It is the perfect way for movie actors to work, but of course it takes time.'

There is no point in trying to refer *To Have and Have Not* to any external reality, except to say that it is a film about two actors falling in love. Bogart wanted to help Bacall, to relax her, so he added to the humour – and ended up easier than he had ever been before. He started looking at her with appreciation. She gave everything back in spades. Mayo Methot lacked the courage to be on set, but she was apprehensive – and anyone of that church knew that such things could happen and were stronger than human laws. Bogart and Bacall were help-less in such a tide. So they started talking, and seeing more of each other and soon he was telling her how unhappy he was. Some may have questioned her oppor-tunism and career-making. But why shouldn't she believe in her luck and smile to think how narrowly she had escaped the attention of that famous wolf, Howard, her director and proprietor?

To Have and Have Not was a big hit. It was nominated for nothing, because in 1944 it seemed silly or marginal. Today, it's easier to see how it is a greater artistic achieve-ment than *Casablanca* just because that silliness was the true heart of the Hollywood movie. It is a film that transcends the war *Casablanca* believes in: it is a film about talk, and looking and desire – it is a tribute to fantasy, and next to money that was all Hollywood believed in. The marriage to Mayo Methot was over – not without scenes, recriminations and Bogart in tears.

The partnership of Bogart and Bacall in life and on the screen was established. And as such dreams go, they were lucky: their best was still to come – for *The Big Sleep* is greater even than *To Have and Have Not*.

Not that Bogart was extended as an actor, or made to work hard. Far from it. The truth is simpler and more profound. He was relaxed. He was able to feel not just that this wise child in his arms was his (for a moment), but that she made him look great, eternal and natural. All at once you could see how Humphrey had always been a little shy and tense and grim in pictures. Now, two films – hard-boiled paradises – found his secret place, the tight corner where he was at ease, and catered to his chronic desire just to look good. All those years of hacking his way through guy films was over. Ida Lupino, Ingrid Bergman and now Bacall had made it clear: the secret to Bogart was a tenderness that he had once feared to reveal. With that lock sprung, the women of the world adored him. His new contract established him as the highest paid actor in pictures. For a guaranteed $200,000 a year, for fifteen years, he had to make just one picture a year at Warners, with time off for another picture somewhere else. In 1946, his earnings were over $400,000 from movies.

This was grand, and it came from hard negotiations from Sam Jaffe his agent. But it shows the conservative in Bogart. By 1946, there were a few actors with much wider ambitions: they wanted to produce their own pictures and take a lot more of the money. Bogart would get a taste for such work himself, but not in 1946. He was content still to be a studio contract player – for fifteen years, no less! If he lived that long.

Like Rick, Bogart preferred to be apart from politics. Yet Rick had served in the Spanish Civil War, we learn. And on a few occasions Bogart had been identified with what were known as left-wing causes. In the 30s he had supported striking lettuce pickers in the San Joaquin Valley and newspaper writers in Seattle. He was unaware of it, but the FBI had a file on him in which it was reckoned that Bogart had 'strong CP leanings'. Then in the summer of 1940, Martin Dies and the House Un-American Activities Committee (HUAC) had taken Bogart on, and been whipped in public.

HUAC was fairly quiet during the war, and America came to recognize Humphrey Bogart as one of its model figures in the conflict. He had done his bit in life (or in Naples), and he had helped crystallize American dreams on the screen – wasn't there a bonus for that kind of national service? It's clear that Bogart prized that reputation. He was often cynical in public and dismissive of lofty causes, but I hope I've made clear how far his effectiveness on screen had to do with the self-image he desired, that of a righteous outsider who grudgingly lent himself to common causes. And in 1946–7, that desire would trap him in a battle he reckoned he had won already.

He was a liberal. He took an interest in the world, he

was American – at that moment, he and Ronald Reagan, say, could mutter all the same clichés in unison. He was not a Communist – though he had the right to be – and it's unlikely that any of his close friends were party members. Still, as HUAC drew itself together again after the war – under the chairmanship of first John Rankin and then J. Parnell Thomas – Bogart sniffed the old fight in which he had won a round.

In the spring of 1947, HUAC ordered preliminary hearings to be held in Los Angeles at which such noted figures as Jack Warner and Louis B. Mayer, Robert Taylor and Gary Cooper, showed every inclination to toe the Committee line. Yes, there were Reds in the picture business, it was said, and yes the pictures were sometimes un-American because of it. Only idiocy and an inability to test evidence could sustain those impressions in public, but 1947 was a new, fearful world. Film is not a business with academic, let alone moral, entry requirements. It takes fools and scoundrels. Over forty film-makers (writers, directors and producers) were subpoenaed to testify in Washington DC in the fall.

Whereupon, a sentiment developed in some Hollywood people that this witch-hunting was absurd, against the law and destructive of confidence or civic duties. A group of names gathered to contest the matter, and Bogart and Bacall were quickly identified as leaders – as much because of their status as because they were actual organizers. There was a Committee for the First Amendment established. It declared that the DC hearings were morally wrong because:

'Any investigation into the political beliefs of the individual is contrary to the basic principles of our democracy.

'Any attempt to curb freedom of expression and to set arbitrary standards of Americanism is in itself disloyal to both the spirit and the letter of the Constitution.'

They were correct in every detail, and there is still some legal dispute as to whether or not the targets of HUAC would have been better advised to claim protection under the First Amendment than take the Fifth. But Bogart was about to learn that being right on screen in a story was a very different thing from mastering uneasy popular opinion in the real America.

A group of stars decided to fly to Washington to attend the hearings. Howard Hughes provided an aircraft and Bogart and Bacall were the photogenic spearheads of a group that also included Paul Henreid, Danny Kaye, John Huston, Evelyn Keyes, Jane Wyatt and Larry Adler. There were other sympathizers – Gene Kelly, Judy Garland, Edward G. Robinson, Frank Sinatra – who couldn't make the flight (or the full exposé of publicity). But the group that did travel was strong and big enough to attract attention – and pressure. The right-wing press began to attack them and from within the industry came talk that they could be threatening their careers. Bogart had plans to form his own producing company with Mark Hellinger. They were going to do some Hemingway material. But there was Hellinger telling Bogie that the deal was in jeopardy so long as the actor was involved in the HUAC protests. Most of the time, Hellinger acted like his own master and a tough New York journalist. But a career was a career; it was a vulnerability.

In the event, no one behaved well. Some of the HUAC witnesses were craven, some shot off their mouths. There was no system to their defence, no wit and no great intelligence – of course, you had to be there, under fire, to know how tough it was to be under pressure without benefit of writers. The industry was cowardly: after a few hesitant steps towards liberalism, it showed itself ready to let HUAC do as it wished. And Bogart decided that he had been used and made a fool of. We don't know the exact form of the pressure put upon him, but realize that Bogart was only lately in the big money. He had bought a yacht, the *Santana*, for $50,000, and he had his own production company with the same name. Blacklisting was becoming a reality. And so most of the big names climbed down, and asked America to see that they were just kids at this new game.

The Hearst press had refused to advertise *Treasure of the Sierra Madre*, and pressure cut away at the box-office revenue on *Dark Passage*. Bogart became very afraid that he might have to go back to the theatre. By the end of 1947, he issued a statement to the effect that while he still denied any Communist associations, 'I went to

Washington because I thought fellow Americans were being deprived of their constitutional rights, and for that reason alone. That the trip was ill-advised, even foolish, I am very ready to admit. At the time it seemed like the right thing to do. I have absolutely no use for Commies nor for anyone who serves that philosophy. I am an American. And very likely, like a good many of you, sometimes a foolish and impetuous American.'

Some on the left – Larry Adler for one – were disgusted by Bogart's cave-in. Of course, we know now, as Bogart did not, just how many people suffered in terms of career, health, family cohesion and even life expectancy. Bogart may have believed that the matter was bigger than he was, or far more intricate. But it was not. He had been right, in his instincts, and he was just a part of the larger weakness in Hollywood. Some say that Bogart never forgave himself, and the details of the period stress how long he waited before changing his mind, and how cynical he became thereafter. It is a classic and distressing example of the difficulty we have in distinguishing and reconciling real heroism or character from their aspiring gestures in fiction.

Bogart and Bacall were married on 21 May 1945 on the farm of his friend Louis Bromfield. It was a simple affair, and apparently done in unfettered happiness – the smile on Bogart's face in the photographs is such as you will find nowhere else. But the break with Mayo Methot had been tortured and prolonged. Bogart clearly felt for this wife and their turbulent times together. He knew she had no career ahead of her and he could hardly argue at her maudlin predictions of what was to come (she died in 1952, in Oregon, of alcoholism). She could make him feel guilty – and he was vulnerable to that emotion. He also reckoned he was amazingly lucky to get Bacall – a knockout, a woman with sophistication way beyond her years and now an actress with earning powers. Alas, the sensation of *To Have and Have Not* came out with her second film – *The Confidential Agent*, with Charles Boyer – and she was quite properly roasted for her wooden, or frozen, performance.

It was not just logical, but necessary that Warners put the married couple together in a new Howard Hawks picture. Hawks may have been wistful over a lost contest, but time would tell this truth – that the only director who could actually make Bacall look at home in pictures was Howard Hawks. Perhaps you didn't have to be a genius to guess that the Hawksian method applied to Raymond Chandler's *The Big Sleep* would be plain sailing. But then you'd have to be ready to explain how it is that Hawks turns a film noir mystery into a screwball love story so that the sequences of blinding intrigue are shuffled together with riotous love scenes like the amazing, musical development in which the two of them call the local police on the telephone.

These were natural assets: the lovely inexplicable Chandler plot; the noir recreation of a shady LA on sets; the thundery music by Max Steiner; the way Sid

Hickox would let light fall on the length of Bacall's hair – to say nothing of a supporting cast that went from Martha Vickers to Dorothy Malone, from Elisha Cook Jr to John Ridgely, and never lets a dull moment survive. It is a film about the happiness of two lovers together before anything like staleness or habit has set in. It is a lesson that such bliss can exist, and it is – I think – the film that most Bogart people would cling on to at the day of judgement. There's no need in a book of this length to say more than that it is a great movie – but it is, and is still as fresh as a Meyer lemon picked from the tree. Taste it. Not to be too crude or fancy about it, it hardly matters what Bogart and Bacall were like in bed – we can hope for the best. What is beyond dispute is that on screen they were the tops. And the Bogart I am offering to you is a man who was himself much persuaded by image and reputation.

Of course, you know that this story has not much more than another ten years to run. Bogart and Bacall were unaware of that, even if he sometimes warned her about the age gap between them. They had children to bridge it, or ignore it, and Bogart seems never to have dreamed of having children before. On 7 January 1949, they had a son, Stephen, named after the name Bacall's character had given Bogart in *To Have and Have Not* – this Harry Morgan was 'Steve' to her, the private name Nancy Hawks kept for Howard. On 23 August 1952, they had a daughter, Leslie Howard, named to honour the actor who had given Bogart that first chance in *The Petrified Forest*.

Still, nothing was perfect. Bogart's prospective partner, Mark Hellinger, dropped dead of a heart attack in
1947 and thus the chance of a series of Hemingway films
came to an end. Ironically, Bogart had already done so
well with a Hemingway travesty. And while Bogart had
his rock-solid contract with Warners, he knew that it
relied upon a hitherto stupid or lucky studio coming up
with the right parts. He made *Conflict* in 1945, *Dead Reck-
oning* in 1947 and *The Two Mrs Carrols* in 1947 (the last a
Hellinger production). They are dull, fabricated, unin-
spired and as routine as *The Big Sleep* is unique. The studio
put Bogart and Bacall together again in *Dark Passage* with
a decent director (Delmer Daves) and a nice gimmicky
story – Bogart escapes from prison and has surgery to
change his face. Truth to tell, it's another film that leaves
you certain how much the easy flexing of *The Big Sleep* –
its turning inside and outside, on the spot – had been just
Hawks. Bogart faced the condition he had known in the
30s: it was probably better to be a star than a supporting
player, but you were always at the mercy of the system,
unless you had the wit or the providence to know and
trust the right people. After *Dark Passage*, Bogart would
make another nineteen pictures. Of those, four or five
are keepers that anyone can still see with profit and pleas-
ure. And one is as good as anything he ever did. The others are humdrum or worse. We are talking about a man
who made four great pictures in his life.

As many as that?

*   *   *

The man is named Fred C. Dobbs and he is the bitter salt of the earth, a small-time cheat and heel, as full of self-pity as spite. He is a character part, and the one member in a central trio where the audience would like the other two guys far better. And it says a great deal about Bogart's openness to new and different parts – to heavies, even – that he was prepared to abandon toupee and likeability for *The Treasure of the Sierra Madre*. The one pressing reason was obvious – John Huston, the effective designer of the Bogart of the 1940s, and the director with whom he was most at ease personally.

B. Traven's novel was published in 1927, and in the years since it had stayed in print and gradually fostered the mysterious reputation of Traven, an author very shy of personal appearance. Huston loved the book and he was going to film it for Warners years earlier, when war broke out. The project was shelved because Huston accepted Traven's feeling – expressed in letters between them – that much of the filming would have to be done in Mexico. Still, the studio kept the property aside for Huston, and he sent Traven a script as early as 1940. Traven liked it but made a few suggestions that the director adopted. There was not much to fight about: Huston and Traven had just the same feeling for Mexico as a picaresque casino with snakes and bandits, a place where adventurers were on their own facing a test of character as to whether you could handle winning or losing without letting them show.

For Huston, the picture became something out of

Treasure of the Sierra Madre, with Walter Huston

the ordinary once they reached Mexico. A man named Hal Croves began visiting the set – nondescript, poorly dressed – and the word spread that it might be Traven. Huston himself never quite made up his mind about this. Henry Blanke was producing, with Ted McCord in charge of photography. The script was set, but still once they were in Mexico Huston became a slave to the real place and its light. He allowed a little enlargement of the script as they went along. The budget began to edge upwards.

There were introductory scenes in Tampico, actually shot on the Warners back lot, where Bobby Blake, the young Robert Blake, played a kid. He watched Bogart with the doting gaze of an apprentice.

I used to watch him like a kid watches a father. You know, you watch your father shave so you can learn how to shave. Bogie used to take his script to the dressing room and there he would read lines into the mirror. I would watch him with the door open a crack; I was like two feet tall; nobody was going to pay attention to me scouting around there. He'd look in the mirror and he'd get a line and he'd rub his ear. Another time he'd do something with his lip. And then he'd take out a pencil and cross out a couple of lines . . . I was fascinated by him cutting his dialogue. I thought, 'Wow, he doesn't want to talk.'

Bogart was not alone – the line stretches from Cagney and Cooper to McQueen and Eastwood – of actors in talking pictures desperate to get every line as lean and hard as possible. And there's good reason: small talk and loose words sound alarms on screen – they give the game away and destroy suspense. Bogart was articulate and well-read, not to mention educated. But it is his essence on screen to seem grudging with every word. Whatever he says seems hard-earned, and not to be missed.

On the other hand, there are scenes where Dobbs really breaks down. Observers on the set then saw a very different Bogart. He was so worked up for these scenes of delusion that at the end of every take he needed time to 'come down', groaning and flapping his arms. Bogart was far from a Method actor and not easily tempted to show his craft, but Dobbs *in extremis* was a greater task than he had ever faced before. Bacall was with him on location, but the film has not a female role, and in the body of the picture Dobbs is increasingly alienated from the other two men – Tim Holt and Walter Huston. Paranoid in life, Dobbs is a role that puts any actor under strain. And there were times when even the affable Huston could be tough with his old friend. Once, they struggled together, and Lauren Bacall had to beg Huston to stop. The director was a bigger man and he had been a boxer. Moreover, Bogart was playing with his real hair, and it was falling out. He looks like a character actor, not a star.

There's a moment early in the film where, just barbered, Bogart looks sleek and sinister, his thin hair lying flat on his head. But then, for most of the story, he's bearded and dishevelled and wearing a hat to cover his departing hair. The brush in the film is broad and vigorous: there was nothing neurotic about Huston, though he could see the neurosis and worse in Dobbs. It's still a classic. When he first saw it, Jack Warner said it was 'definitely the greatest motion picture we have ever made. It is really one that we have always wished for.'

But at 124 minutes, it was a strain for a public set on romance. One woman in the mining group might have made a lot of difference – sure, Huston could have responded, it would have ruined it. The real problem was that six months or so in Mexico had pushed the budget over $3 million. It's not quite clear why, with the small cast and not much action. But that was a heavy burden for a male picture. It was at the Academy that it was recognized. John Huston won for his screenplay and direction. The film was nominated as Best Picture. And Walter Huston won a very popular Oscar for Best Supporting Actor. He is the heart of the film – he might as well be the lead but for that storytelling spirit that sees no central or star roles in life. Bogart's part was too nasty to be rewarded, but it is arguably the biggest and most complete acting stretch he had taken so far. As such, its very adventurousness makes it feel a touch odd or mannered.

Friends could always try to work together. The best thing about studio employment was that you found sympathetic spirits – Sid Hickox on the camera, Bob Lord producing, or Lorre and Greenstreet to do scenes with. Bogart's best friend in pictures was John Huston, and they had survived the ordeal of the Mexican location well enough. So let's do it again. There would be a role for Bacall, too, so they fell upon *Key Largo* in unison. From Huston's point of view it offered a chance to do some marlin fishing off the Florida Keys – he liked those bonuses and he would do *The African Queen* for the chance to hunt big game.

Key Largo was an oddity, a property Warner Brothers had acquired, but which had defied successful adaptation. It was a play by Maxwell Anderson. There's a prologue in Spain during the Civil War in which King McCloud (played by Paul Muni on Broadway) urges his men to desert the cause. Then years later, McCloud visits the Florida Keys to see the family of one of those men. He finds gangsters on the run threatening the family and he sacrifices himself to save them. It had been a play full of late 30s pessimism about a world beyond rescue.

Huston went to the Keys with a young writer, Richard Brooks, and they laboured over a way to make the material workable for 1948. Of course, they cut Spain. They settled on the idea that McCloud has come by to tell the widow and the father of a fellow-soldier what a great guy and hero they had had. Bacall would be the widow and Lionel Barrymore the father (in a wheelchair). But there at Key Largo, with a storm coming up, the resort hotel the family runs is taken over by gangsters. Edward G. Robinson was their noxious boss. And, of course, McCloud puts it all right: he takes the gangsters out, one by one, and he gives the widow something to live for again. Bogart and Bacall are together, and she is a doe of admiration and obedience to him. It's striking that even someone as smart as Huston couldn't see that Bogart and Bacall were much better sparring than purring, and naturally inclined to comedy. In life, Bogart was famous for teasing or needling, and there were arguments over how mean he was. In life, it's fairly clear that the couple jabbed and shadowboxed, even if they couldn't always keep their own lines Hawksian. Still they knew their natural positioning. And *Key Largo* didn't.

So it's a solemn little tale, easily stolen by Robinson's gangster – Johnny Rocco – squat, sweaty, dirty-minded and relishing it all. There's a moment where Robinson whispers filthy talk in Bacall's fine ear – she shivers like a horse, and we're meant to think how loathsome Rocco is. Nowadays, I suspect it might be more interesting to hear what Rocco said and see what he planned. In his bath, smoking a cigar, Rocco is a reptile – Huston called him 'a crustacean with its shell off'.

Rocco's entourage includes a drunken girl friend, well past her prime. At one point Rocco taunts her into singing the song 'Moanin' Low' in return for a drink. She does the song, struggling, on the edge of humiliation – and then Rocco withdraws the offer of the drink. Claire Trevor got this part and she won the supporting

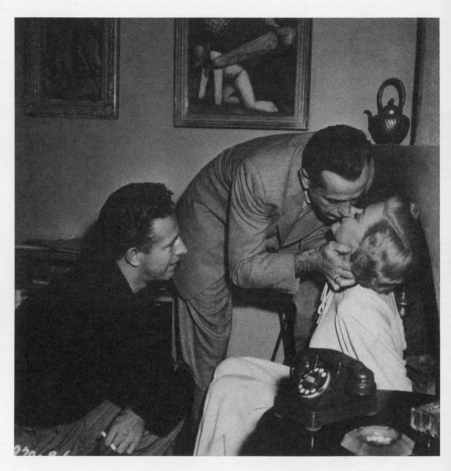

Rehearsing *In A Lonely Place*,
with Nicholas Ray and Gloria Grahame

actress Oscar in it. There is not much else to be said for *Key Largo*. It shows how easily like-minded friends, and a lot of talent, could produce a mediocre picture instead of something fine. Indeed, as it stands *Key Largo* might be a lot more suspenseful without Bogart's McCloud. Suppose that the widow and the crippled father found some desperate way to defeat the gangsters. But suppose one of the gangsters – a half-likeable guy – tells Bacall, come away, you're rotting here, and she kills him, out of duty to law and order but in self-denial. That is a more dangerous situation, and a novel picture.

Of course, there might be new friends, too. Bogart the contract player had been a steady enemy to his studio, and that feeling never abated as he worked on better terms. Stars got screwed, too. Like many established actors in the late 40s, Bogart began to see his need to formulate his own working set-up – he might as well go all the way, pick his material and his associates. It was that or do it yourself, and Bogart never seems to have shown or possessed the extra ambition to direct. So he met Nicholas Ray, clearly one of the most promising newcomers in the post-war Hollywood.

Ray was not a kid; in 1948, he was thirty-seven already. But he was new to pictures. He had a debut – made at R.K.O. for producer John Houseman – called *They Live by Night*. Shot in 1947 but not released until 1949, it was a film people were talking about. Farley Granger played a young member of a gang of criminals living and operating in a rural setting. He is plainly doomed, yet he meets a girl (Cathy O'Donnell) and finds a brief idyll with her before fate closes in. Shot in black-and-white, and made with all the flair and excitement of a young talent fresh to directing, it was by no means a conventional gangster film but a movie that recovered the real people existing under the armour plate of the gangster clichés.

In person, Ray was tall, handsome yet chronically inarticulate. He seemed like a dreamer struggling towards his dream, in a night of intense, neurotic darkness. He was a long shot from the professional studio directors of the 1930s – he might be an artist, or a poseur. As Bogart tried to recover from the unexpected death of Mark Hellinger, so he had to make or pass on a Hellinger project. This was *Knock on Any Door*, about a young urban hoodlum and his defence lawyer. Bogart had always been set to play the lawyer, and once at least Marlon Brando had talked of playing the kid – Nick Romano. Robert Lord, the former Warners producer and the writer of *Black Legion*, was part of the new company. Bogart called it Santana, with a deal for Columbia to distribute. He asked Nick Ray to direct the movie and they cast a very good-looking unknown – John Derek – as Romano.

No one could honestly say *Knock on Any Door* worked. In the moment of Brando, there had been thoughts of getting at a new type of young person after the war. In the event, however, *Knock on Any Door* feels like a throwback to the 1930s with too much soulful lamentation in court on behalf of misunderstood kids. (One day soon, Nick Ray would learn that to explore the new kids it was important to keep the adult roles to a minimum – that was one principle behind *Rebel Without a Cause*.)

In addition, the working relationship between Bogart and Ray was strained. Bogart was brisk, no nonsense. He came in knowing his lines, ready to shoot. Ray was still fumbling towards things he could hardly express. It wasn't a fit and sometimes Bogart had to take Ray aside and give him a quick lesson in how pictures got done. But the more they talked, the better they got along and the more Bogart believed in Ray's vision. Bogart knew he needed young ideas and he was convinced of Ray's irregular traits. Most important of all, as they socialized, they found they were alike: older men with drinking problems and younger wives – Ray had just married the actress Gloria Grahame, who was twenty-four. Bogart and Ray drank, gambled and both worried about what beautiful, flirtatious wives were up to. Ray left observations on his situation, and it's the first signal that Bogart and Bacall might be more or less than the ideal couple in magazine stories.

The four went out together socially and that interaction lay behind the smouldering triumph called *In a Lonely Place*. This came from a novel, by Dorothy Hughes, and a script by Andrew Solt. The central figure, Dixon Steele, is a Hollywood screenwriter – established and a success, but ageing and anxious and convinced that he has prostituted himself. It is also clear that he has a temper and a violent streak, both of which seem driven by his feelings of failure. He has an unhappy love life, but now he meets a new woman, Laurel Gray. This coincides with the death of a young woman and some police suspicion that Dix could be the killer. Laurel helps to clear him. The love builds, but along the way Laurel discovers violence in Dix that might be murderous one day. It is enough to destroy the relationship.

Against initial studio feelings that Ginger Rogers be Laurel, and even a flurry of thinking that Lauren Bacall could play the part, Ray insisted on casting Gloria Grahame – just as their marriage broke down. Was that casting meant to help avert divorce, or was it a final parting gesture? No one can say, but it surely helps account for the remarkable emotional tension in the film. Further, every bit of Hollywood gossip about Bogart's own hostile streak was mined by the situation of the film. Bogart shows anger sometimes in other films, but nowhere else is there such a sense of repressed and coiled malice. Nor is there another film where his inner tension seems such a part of the world – that of movie-making. *In a Lonely Place* is not a direct assault on Hollywood, like *Sunset Blvd* (made in the same year), but it stands up now as a far more probing analysis of the uneasiness of the town. That likely comes from Ray more than from Bogart, but people recalled that as recently as 1940 Bogart had written a magazine article entitled 'Why Hollywood Hates Me'.

Looking at you

In fact, Bogart was increasingly popular, and his image was enhanced by the Bacall love story. But those who had known him recognized the drunken binges, the rancour and the contempt for the sham of Hollywood. What is so startling and frightening about *In a Lonely Place* is the sudden reappearance of this venom and the self-destructive energy behind it. It may count as a self-portrait of Nick Ray, but the public sees the man on screen. The snarl seizes the actor's face. That's one reason why *In a Lonely Place* is regarded as a masterpiece now, while it did only moderate business (enough to slow down plans at Santana).

Ray and Bogart never split, and they had a project together at Warners, *Round Trip*, for which Ray had written or was meant to write an original script. But that collapsed because in the early 50s, finally disgusted with his old studio, Bogart allowed himself to be bought out of the majority of his fifteen-year contract at Warners. Among Ray's later films, one could easily see Bogart in *Bigger Than Life*, as the megalomaniac schoolteacher who is swept away by cortisone (not that James Mason wasn't superb in the role). Above all, Ray had an appetite for people living close to their edge, characters unsettled and likely to crack. This was getting at an energy that very few of Bogart's films really explored. The wonder may be not that the two men did so little together, but that *In a Lonely Place* turned out so well. It has the sudden darkening view in our portrait of a familiar star such as John Wayne allowed in *Red River*, or

Robert Mitchum in *The Night of the Hunter*. Grant that Ray and Bogart extended each other in useful but perilous ways and it may be that Bogart's stature as a star helps account for one of Ray's most enigmatic but coherent views of the creative personality. Incidentally, it is the clearest glimpse we have of that thing in Bogart – call it temper, misanthropy or an uncontrollable urge to needle – that would ride lesser mortals and which became a strange model of behaviour in the Rat Pack (the one manifestation of Bogie-ism that was apparent before his death).

Dixon Steele is the kind of man who gets into night-club scuffles because of his temper, or his reluctance to back off – or just because he's often loaded. By common description, Bogart was 'happy' now: he was in the best of his marriages; he was rich; he was very popular. But the past had left him alcoholic: someone who drinks all the time ends up fitting this medical description. Moreover, after marrying Bacall, his life changed. Mayo Methot had favoured side-alley bars for her drinking. Bacall liked parties, celebrities and fun – it was what she had bought into by marrying a much older star. So they went out a lot more than Bogart was used to. They socialized. They had a circle – by and large it was composed of successful showbiz people, tough, cynical, boozy, flirtatious and disdainful of Hollywood. Frequent members of the group were Nunnally Johnson, a writer-producer, Spencer Tracy, John Huston, David Niven, Mike Romanoff, Swifty Lazar and

Frank Sinatra. It's plain that Sinatra adored Bogart and took him as a model – the star as a bit of a gangster. In Frank's great years he had a peaked toupee that might have come from Bogie's wig-maker. He had Bogart's wisecracks on his lips. He liked to be respected as a tough guy. And he often had Lauren Bacall on his arm. Hard-drinking, unsentimental, as worldly as they could manage, they called themselves a rat pack. In the event, Bogart's early death, and his heroic way of dealing with it, became further emblems of the rat code. It was a kind of chivalry.

And sometimes Bogart fought. There were long nights on the town when he was smashed, hostile and ugly. There were jokes mixed in with the malice, but some people were afraid. A good friend, Nunnally Johnson, said 'There are a lot of people who still detest him, people he had deliberately affronted, and God knows he could do that viciously'. When Bacall was away, Bogart often moved in with his expert wig-maker, Venetia Peterson.

Not everything went smoothly. As Warner Brothers prepared to film Ayn Rand's novel, *The Fountainhead*, there was some thought – not least from Ms Rand herself – that Humphrey Bogart was unique among available actors in that he seemed to have access to the intellect, the hard-nosed eloquence and the authority required in Howard Roark the wilful genius architect. Bogart was very interested. But director King Vidor saw the rather more obvious architecture in Gary

Cooper – tall, upright, heroic – and Bogart lost out. At much the same time, he tried to purchase the film rights for Santana in Sidney Kingsley's play *Detective Story* which opened in 1949. The central figure of that play was a fanatical detective whose life breaks down under the complex demands of his job. It was a novel vision of the strains of a police life. Ralph Bellamy had played the part on stage, and when a film emerged, with William Wyler directing, Kirk Douglas stepped forward in the lead part.

On the other hand, Santana went forward with a second-rate war film, *Tokyo Joe*, and then for Warners he made *Chain Lightning*, in which he is a wartime flyer who becomes a test pilot. Then in 1951 he came out with two more duds – *Sirocco* (set in Syria in the 1920s) and *The Enforcer*, a complete throwback to Warners of the 1930s in which he is a DA trying to dismantle organized crime. With Raoul Walsh as a co-director, *The Enforcer* is the best of this group of films, but it was based on the assumption that Bogart was fit for routine work – like John Wayne, say. This was not so. Bogart was ageing before America's eyes and he was aching for character. He needed rescue again.

C.S. Forester's *The African Queen* had been published in 1935, and straightaway there were thoughts that a movie version might be ideal for Charles Laughton and his wife Elsa Lanchester. A little later, Warners had looked at it as a Bette Davis project – with David Niven. But the rights became free again, and with the enthusiastic support of John Huston, the producer Sam Spiegel raised enough money to buy them. From the very start, Huston dreamed of putting Bogart together with Katharine Hepburn as Charlie Allnut and Rose Sayer, the rat and the swan who take the creaking old steamboat, *The African Queen*, against a German gunboat.

Huston made it clear that he planned to shoot in Africa, and no one underestimated the hardships in that. But Bogart was persuaded to take the part – an Englishman, a lower-class character part – if only because he had never been offered a sweeter deal. Spiegel made an alliance of his own Horizon Pictures with the British company, Romulus – this would permit the use of sterling tied up in British East Africa. Bogart was to get $125,000 deferred against 30 per cent of the profits. He had never had such a generous back-end offer. Hepburn was to get $65,000 up front, another $65,000 deferred against 10 per cent of the profits, and as for Huston, he was supposed to get 50 per cent of the profits. The only disconcerting thing about this fulsome deal was the wondering why Spiegel – a famously devious operator – was content with so little.

But as Spiegel might have sighed, let's shoot the picture first. *The African Queen* did go to East Africa. Huston hired James Agee to do a script and after Agee had proved disabled by drink Peter Viertel was called in to rescue it. Jack Cardiff handled the Technicolor photography, Wilfrid Shingleton ran the art direction, and the

The African Queen, with Katharine Hepburn

two stars weathered the place, the climate and each other. Bogart did not really bother to play Allnut as English so much as low and raucous. After initial difficulties, where she made Rose too officious and disapproving, Huston guided Hepburn into a ladylike interpretation of Rose based on Eleanor Roosevelt.

The picture is untouchable, in great part because its germ was a timeless love story for unexpected opposites – in defiance of every movie executive who had failed to see the potential there in nearly fifteen years. It's a comedy and a love story, with benefit of a wartime situation and all the natural splendour of Africa. This was not the Africa of handsome natives and safari views of animals (as in *King Solomon's Mines*), it was the Africa of jungle, river, insects and leeches. And in 1951, the rigour of the location was a big part of the film's appeal. Forester himself had had different endings in the past – happy and unhappy – but Huston settled for sweet irony letting the Allnut–Sayer plans work out. Bogart was able to battle his lady, and Hepburn the feminist was given one more story in which she ended up serving her man. It seemed old-fashioned in 1951 (though Africa in colour offset that), but it also resounded as a triumph of middle-aged cinema.

The picture cost its two companies a little over a million dollars: despite Africa it was a very small story. From the outset, it was a picture that the public loved. Spiegel was going for rentals of $3 million. But in the event the film went over $4 million. In the past, Bogart had often belittled the Oscars, but he snapped to attention when he was nominated for Charlie Allnut. His competition could hardly have been tougher – Fredric March in *Death of a Salesman*, Arthur Kennedy in *Bright Victory*, Montgomery Clift in *A Place in the Sun* and Marlon Brando in *A Streetcar Named Desire*. In addition, Hepburn was nominated, along with Huston for directing, and Huston and Agee for screenplay. It therefore seemed bizarre – and a jab at Sam Spiegel – that the film was not nominated for Best Picture. When Bogart won, he was there and he was grateful. More than that, he decided that acting could be taken more seriously.

The money did not work out as well. As the picture sailed into profit, Huston and Bogart both discovered delays in the proceeds, and then the possibility of errors or worse in the accounting. It dragged on, and Huston was compelled (by gambling debts) to settle for a pittance. As for Bogart, the facts are not quite clear. By any stretching of the numbers, *The African Queen* was about $2 million in profit, and the actor was set to get $600,000 of that. Morgan Maree, his business manager, did all he could. But Spiegel was slippery. Still, it is likely that *The African Queen* secured Bogart's fortune and an eventual estate that stood at over $1 million.

The lesson sank in again: after your biggest hits and most unfettered work, you could look lost again. Out of friendship for the writer Richard Brooks, Bogart took on two pictures with him in a row – *Deadline – U.S.A.*

and *Battle Circus*, the first about an attempt to save a worthy newspaper in a changing world, and the second about a military hospital in the Korean War (does that ring any bells?) with Bogart as a surgeon falling for a nurse played by June Allyson. This was 1951 and 53, and at much the same time Ms Allyson was a smash hit as the wife in *The Glenn Miller Story*. Good for her. Still, she is not quite the actress one dreams of playing opposite Bogart. Of the two Brooks films, *Deadline – U.S.A.* is far the superior with some strong supporting performances (Ethel Barrymore, Ed Begley, Paul Stewart). Yet in truth they both show a film industry beginning to lose confidence and contact with the public in an age of television.

It was in something of this spirit that the great chums, Huston and Bogart, came to their Waterloo. Not that *Beat the Devil* is simply a defeat, or a film without entertainment values. It looks more clearly now like one of the first pictures based on the idea of parodying certain kinds of Hollywood classic. In short, it's a satire at a moment when only the reckless, the bored and the moderns could see such an opening. It's as if a dozen years later, Huston had come out of a hangover and thought to himself, what if the characters or the types from *The Maltese Falcon* all teamed up again in the new crazy Europe? It's not a feeble idea, and it's a beguiling film. But it was a disaster.

The whole thing was Huston's doing. A neighbour of his in Ireland, Claud Cockburn, had published a novel,

Beat the Devil, and Huston asked Bogie to buy it — cheaply, not a real burden. The falcon this time was a uranium mine and the people after it were a motley crew: Billy Dannreuther and his lustrous but not terribly bright wife (Bogart and some fabulous continental sexpot to be named later); two classic villains, Greenstreet and Lorre — except that Greenstreet was dead. So Robert Morley took over. Lorre was not well either but alive enough to be himself and so anxious to be reunited with Bogart that he took the job for peanuts. There was also an English couple, him stupid, her crazy. The two big female roles ended up as Gina Lollobrigida and a blonde Jennifer Jones. And the idea was to shoot it all in Italy. What was missing were Sam Spade and his moral resolve. All players in the game were now on the same slippery slope.

It's possible that Huston was still smarting from the money he'd lost on *The African Queen*. It's possible that he felt Bogart relied on him. There were some on the crowded picture who got the idea that Huston and Bogart had a buried enmity: that Bogart envied Huston his blithe charm and his ability to pick up any woman; while Huston was resentful of the money. Whatever the reality, Huston took a big fee ($175,000) to direct and produce and proceeded to run Santana into the red. All seemed well. Huston sent Bogie a note proposing how Billy should look: 'Not that old thing that's been haunting raincoats and snap-brimmed hats for God knows how long. I'd like to see you as a very Continental type fellow – an extreme figure in a homburg, shoulders unpadded, French cuffs, regency trousers fancy waistcoats and a walking stick.'

Was that badinage, or needling? Was it even a suggestion that Bogie act a little gay? At which point I have to say that an underground legend persists to the effect that in his youth and his theatre days Bogart had been bisexual. Bogart responded to Huston's suggestion brusquely though he admitted he was sick of the trenchcoat himself. It's hard to be sure about the innuendo, just as on the set of the film it was often hard to know what was happening. As well as arm-wrestling Bogie, Truman Capote was doing the script night by night with the result that it is fitful, funny but fragmented. Too many visitors were around for concentration. Almost at Huston's instigation, the film was a party. It was as if he had planned the mess. If that sounds fanciful, then the reader may need to be better acquainted with the caprice of John Huston, a man whose religion was gambling.

When he had edited the picture, Huston wrote to Bogart, hoping that it might be a success, but 'it cost hellishly. However, if the humor comes off – as I pray it will – I believe it will make some very tidy sums. On the other hand, if the joke should fall flat – well, God help us!'

Bogart had put $400,000 of his own money into the film, and it never came back. It was at this time that he began to feel weary. Yet he stepped up his work rate, as if anxious about the future.

Nothing he did in these last years meant as much to him as Lieutenant-Commander Queeg in *The Caine Mutiny*. It was a character part and a heavy, and it was a role that Bogart and his earlier naval history took very seriously. He wore the toupee still, but he was able to look older. For instance, Bogart was only nine years older than Fred MacMurray who appears in the same film as Lieutenant Tom Keefer. Yet the gap between them seems far greater. Bogart's face was fleshier, his eyes more anxious. It was noted by friends that he was suffering from apparent indigestion and was chewing on tablets against it much of the time.

Herman Wouk's *The Caine Mutiny* had been published in 1951, and it won a generous Pulitzer Prize. Captain Queeg was said to be a widely sought-after part, and Bogart actually attended his audition rolling ball bearings in his hand, like the character. He made it clear to Columbia, the studio, that he'd work for less than his usual rate to get the part – then he griped about the stingy deal later. But it's hard now to see what made Queeg so desirable. For most of the book, he is depicted as a querulous martinet, without inner life or justification. Then in a very stagy court martial he goes through a spectacular and convenient breakdown only to be effectively exonerated by the officer who defended the men who mutinied against Queeg. It is said that Queeg was just the wretched, flawed heart of the Navy doing his best. But there's no other way to play the part really than as a paranoid begging to be exposed.

It's plain that Bogart had thought about this role carefully, but care is a million miles from naturalness. He brings out the Queegian tricks – the clichés of speech, the twitch, the ball bearings – as if under instruction. I think the task may be beyond any actor because of Wouk's writing. But somehow Queeg needs to be made human and plausible. He needs a life beyond the wretched ship he runs. Another approach to the film might have given him a home life – an invalid wife, an autistic child, a pain he needs to escape? Better we have that than the boring love life of a young ensign on the *Caine*.

Bogart is allowed no charm or subtlety under Edward Dmytryk's direction, but the film is like a big ship moving ponderously and slow to shift in its course. The film cannot have it both ways – and Queeg is plainly unfit for command. The court martial has no real reason for being there unless it is to vindicate mutiny and have Queeg's twisted soul exposed. A deeper rift in Bogart might have been so much more interesting – suppose Queeg is reticent, charming, gently artful at coaxing others towards his point of view. But once it is clear that Queeg is about to let the *Caine* founder, and is a naked coward, then there is no doubt about the decision to overthrow his command. There needs to be doubt over the court's decision if Queeg is to remain an intriguing figure.

Bogart was nominated for an Oscar (he lost to Marlon Brando in *On the Waterfront*), just as the lumbering picture was nominated for Best Picture. All of which only testifies to the excessive respect for literary ventures in the 50s. We know all too well what Queeg is going to do and say in advance. That is what ruins the film. But Bogart had thought deeply about Queeg's illness: 'I don't know whether he was a schizophrenic, a manic depressive or a paranoiac – ask a psychiatrist – but I do know that a person who has any one of these things works overtime at being normal. In fact he's super normal until pressured. And then he blows up. I personally know a Queeg in every studio . . .'

At the time, *The Barefoot Contessa* was regarded as a very important picture. Nearly every actress in the world fancied herself as the barefoot gypsy girl taken up in the movie world. And, of course, writer-director Joseph L. Mankiewicz had an armful of Oscars to demonstrate his biting intelligence (or was it just smart dialogue?). Alas, *The Barefoot Contessa* is a dreary, prolonged film, too timid to be as shocking as it wishes, too complacent to uncover the real horrors of café society spending time with movie people.

It appeared as if Bogart had the lead role – Harry Dawes, the ex-alcoholic writer-director who starts to tell the story of Maria Vargas from the crowd at her funeral – it is a great start by Jack Cardiff, a screen full of soaked black umbrellas clustered round an ornate white grave. That is the end of cinematic excitement. Dawes is a storyteller with far less to do than Nick Carraway has in *The Great Gatsby*. As a result, he quickly becomes the rueful wiseacre who tells us everything and does nothing. If anyone thought this portrait of Hollywood on the loose in Europe was scandalous, they hadn't seen *In a Lonely Place*, let alone *Sunset Blvd*.

The Barefoot Contessa is tame and stately, a terrible combination, and Maria is a monotonously nice girl. If only she could have been as volatile as Ava Gardner! Bogart looks tired and morose. On the set, he did not get on with Gardner because the Bogarts were so close to the Frank Sinatra who had been dumped by Ava. Mankiewicz and Bogart got into a battle of wills that the director won. And for the first time, apparently, Bogart's cough was a serious intrusion on filming. He was smoking unfiltered Chesterfields all the time and he could not stop coughing. What the picture needed for Bogart was a plot twist where the sour know-all Dawes himself went crazy for Maria in the end, abandoning all his accumulated wisdom and detachment to make a fool of himself one last time – the droning narrator croaks! But Mankiewicz never imagined it, and the lament goes on without a break. (Dawes stays sedately married to the English actress Elizabeth Sellars.) Only one Oscar accrued to the venture: the supporting actor award for Edmond O'Brien's over-the-top press agent.

Bacall was in Rome for some of *The Barefoot Contessa* shoot, but she does not seem to have noticed Bogart's coughing. We know too little about his eventual cancer to be sure but clearly this was a moment when he didn't seek out the best doctors.

But he was working hard – did he have some intuition? Alas, he plunged into another disappointing picture, *Sabrina*, for Billy Wilder, in which he would play the rather solemn businessman brother, Linus Larrabee, who, like his playboy brother, falls for the chauffeur's daughter when she proves to be Audrey Hepburn. Bogart blamed it on pacts between Wilder and Hepburn and Wilder and William Holden (the playboy), but this was a very bad-tempered production in which audiences were asked to buy an ending in which the girl – one of the great girls of the 1950s – falls for a man not just old enough to be her father, but grumpy enough to be the grandfather. Wilder was a fierce wit and a terrific fighter and he never liked Bogart, especially when the actor started making flagrant anti-German 'jokes'. There came a day when Wilder told him, 'I examine your face, Bogie, your ugly face, and I know that somewhere underneath the sickening face of a shit – is a real shit.' Bogart responded by keeping strict hours, walking off the set at 6 p. m. whatever was happening, and being cool with co-workers. He believed all along that Wilder had wanted Cary Grant for the Linus part – probably true, wouldn't you? In film after film now, Bogart was superfluous baggage and a problem on the set.

There would be four more films: *We're No Angels*, reunited with Michael Curtiz, co-starring Peter Ustinov and Aldo Ray – a comedy; *The Left Hand of God* – a thankless melodrama set in China, co-starring Gene Tierney, with Bogart playing a priest. And then *The*

Desperate Hours, a play about a middle-class household taken over by gangsters on the run. Bogart was his last gangster, Glenn Griffin, and he rose to the challenge. He had hoped to have Spencer Tracy opposite him as the man of the household, but their agents could not agree on billing. So Fredric March got that part. With William Wyler directing, it's a decent suspense picture with Bogie happy to turn on the nasties again. And then finally, *The Harder They Fall*, a boxing movie, where Bogart plays the press writer who sees the corruption of the business and tries to save a new fighter, Toro Moreno, from being exploited. A young Rod Steiger played the hateful fight promoter and there are cruel scenes where he quite deliberately out-acts with Bogart. It's not a good film, but it has a coat of varnished honesty and Bogart looks like a wreck.

Some time quite early in 1956, Bogart bumped into Greer Garson. She heard his cough and was so alarmed she took him to see her doctor on the spot. That man thought he found inflammation of the oesophagus and called for tests. 'I was so used to Bogie's cough,' Lauren Bacall would write later, 'that I hadn't been aware of a change.' Bogart had trouble eating. They went to Palm Springs for a rest – at Sinatra's house – when the doctors announced that surgery would be necessary. On 29 February 1956 he went to the Good Samaritan Hospital in Los Angeles to have his oesophagus removed. But the operation took far longer than was advised. There

In a lonely place

were signs that the cancer had spread and Bogart was advised to take a thorough course of chemotherapy. He was losing weight fast and he had lost his appetite. Gradually, the word got around that he was a dying man.

As much as possible, he was kept at home, and as he shrank and as his energy vanished so the dumb waiter was used to get him upstairs and downstairs. But he liked to be present at cocktail hour and there were friends who wanted to come by. It was in this time that he grew very close to Spencer Tracy, and Tracy and Hepburn were the most frequent visitors at the house. It was clear at last that the bad moods in the man could be resolved into great courage and stoicism. He was taken to the *Santana* occasionally, but it was more than he could handle. Near the end John Huston returned from shooting *Moby Dick* off Ireland, and he called at the house. In the time he'd been away, his friend was wasted:

The cords of his neck stood out, and his eyes were enormous in his gaunt face. Betty decided not to tell Bogie the truth of his condition. I'm not sure whether that was the correct choice, but we went along. One night, Betty, Bogie's doctor, Morgan Maree and I were all sitting around in his living room when Bogie said, 'Look, give me the lowdown. You aren't kidding me, are you?' I took a deep breath and held it. The doctor finally assured Bogie that it was the treatments he had undergone that were making him feel badly, and lose weight. Now that he was off the treatments, he should improve rapidly. Then we all chimed in compounding the falsehood. He seemed to accept it.

Just weeks after his fifty-seventh birthday, on 14 January 1957, Bogart died.

The impact was extraordinary. There had been press warnings, but the family denied them. And Humphrey Bogart was a young man. There was a way in which old Hollywood was just about to learn the habit of funerals. In the few years after Bogart's death, these people died: Erich von Stroheim, Oliver Hardy, Louis B. Mayer, Ronald Colman, Robert Donat, Tyrone Power, Cecil B. DeMille, Ethel Barrymore, Preston Sturges, Errol Flynn, Margaret Sullavan, Clark Gable, Gary Cooper, Marion Davies, Michael Curtiz. And it was still only 1962. A range of people glibly called 'immortal' were to discover that no exception had been made for them. The confidence in the movies has never been the same again.

Bogart had wanted to be cremated and have his ashes scattered in the Pacific from the *Santana*. But that was against the law and so there was a memorial service on 18 January. 'Everyone' was there – except for Howard Hawks: that friendship had died. Nunnally Johnson, David Niven, Mike Romanoff, Leland Hayward and Irving Lazar were ushers. There was a reading from Tennyson, a passage about sailing, 'Crossing the Bar'. Spencer Tracy had been asked, but he believed it was beyond him. So John Huston read a eulogy:

With the years he had become increasingly aware of the dignity of his profession – Actor, not Star: Actor. Himself, he never took too seriously – his work most seriously. He regarded the somewhat gaudy figure of Bogart, the star, with amused cynicism; Bogart, the actor, he held in deep respect . . . Those who did not know him well, who never worked with him, who were not of the small circle of his close friends, had another completely different take on the man than the few who were so privileged. I suppose the ones who knew him but slightly were at the greatest disadvantage, particularly if they were the least bit solemn about their importance. Bigwigs have been known to stay away from the brilliant Hollywood occasions rather than expose their swelling neck muscles to Bogart's banderillas . . .

The legend soon enough takes over from the facts in such situations. There are plenty of books on Humphrey Bogart now, including a good biography by A.M. Sperber and Eric Lax as well as memoirs by his wife and son. But it was plain that something else was happening in the 60s – not just Jean-Paul Belmondo looking at movie posters and sighing, 'Bogie', at the start of *A Bout de Souffle*. The younger generation rediscovered Bogart. In repertory theatres there were festivals of Bogart movies, and they became classics in the new age of film literacy.

The man, I suspect, was more complicated and troubled than we will ever know now – and sometimes when that trouble showed – in *In a Lonely Place* – he was a great actor. But he is remembered now for a few films where he never shows trouble and never puts a foot wrong – *Casablanca, To Have and Have Not, The Big Sleep.* He was perfect there in a medium that believed in flawlessness as a dream and found a moment or two where the ease and wit of a graceful man handling pressure could be seen and treasured – he was as serene as Astaire. Without him behaving like a jerk or an idiot. In life, few of us ever enjoy that privilege except for a minute or two here or there. Bogart had six hours or so of rough grace in the age of a war that most people regarded as life or death.

A Note on Sources

'Bogie' or 'Bogey'? The more widely you read about Humphrey Bogart, the more confusion you find – sometimes within the same book. But Lauren Bacall, in *By Myself* (New York, 1979), opts for 'Bogie', and I like to think of the name on her lips and in her letters. *By Myself*, a pretty good book, is a valuable source in this story, second only to *Bogart* (New York, 1997), by A. M. Sperber and Eric Lax, the most thorough of the biographies. Several other books are very helpful: Lawrence Grobel's *The Hustons* (New York, 1989), which is a lot fuller than Huston's own *An Open Book* (New York, 1980). There is also Stephen Bogart's *In Search of My Father* (New York, 1995); Verita Thompson's *Bogie and Me: A Love Story* (New York, 1982); Katharine Hepburn's *The Making of The African Queen* (New York, 1987); and Aljean Harmetz's *Round Up the Usual Suspects: The Making of Casablanca* (New York, 1992).

Picture Credits

Page 9
The Kobal Collection

Page 14
Warner Brothers/The Kobal Collection

Page 18
Warner Bros/The Kobal Collection

Page 34
Warner Bros/The Kobal Collection

Page 46
Mack Elliott/Warner Bros/First National/The Kobal
Collection

Page 56
Jack Woods/Warner Bros/The Kobal Collection

Page 75
Warner Bros/The Kobal Collection

Page 88
Warner Bros/The Kobal Collection

Page 94
Hulton Archive/Getty Images

Page 99
George Hurrell/Warner Bros/The Kobal Collection

Page 105
Romulus/Horizon/The Kobal Collection

Page 117
Popperfoto/Getty Images